How to Become a Successful Student Athlete

By Louisa Warwin

Disclaimer

All the information in this book is to be used for informational and educational purposes only. The author will not account in any way for any results that stem from the use of the contents herein. While conscious and creative attempts have been made to ensure that all information provided herein is as accurate and useful as possible, the author is not legally bound to be responsible for any damage caused by the accuracy as well as use/misuse of this information.

Contents

Introduction

"This is the true athlete—the person in rigorous training against false impressions. Remain firm, you who suffer, don't be kidnapped by your impressions! The struggle is great, the task divine— to gain mastery, freedom, happiness, and tranquility."

—EPICTETUS, DISCOURSES, 2.18.27–28.

Being an athlete is one of the most challenging roles and positions an individual could ever find themselves.

Why do I say this? There is so much required from people with such role than what meets the eye. First, there is the need to be constantly fit, this would ensure that we are ready for whatever our field of focus thrust upon us. So, we throw ourselves in endless workouts and practices; that is, every other area of our life revolves around this position. It's the sport before the person.

As if the pressure we have already put on ourselves is not enough, we take on the expectations our coaches, fans, and families have for us based on all the hours we have put into practice. There is a certain level of result they expect.

However, if you understand an athlete to be someone that only moves based on the expectations of others, then allow me correct you. We are not in this position to entertain or excite spectators. As much as it might be a secondary responsibility, it is not the main thing. Epictetus's opinion of an athlete truly resonates with me, as I view the role of an athlete as something divine. Whether you are on track, vault, beam, or skates, it is a divine call to mastery, freedom, happiness, and tranquility.

I have been figure skating competitively for the past two decades - practically my whole life, it is all I have come to know. Although I have been in this field for the past twenty years, my last six years is something I would like to focus on in this context. It has formed the basis of all that would be shared in this book; a guide for athletes who want to excel while pursuing sports in college.

"If I knew then, what I know now?" I could claim that this was the thought that birthed this book as I realized that I would have made marginally different decisions in my junior and senior years of high school if I had an appropriate guide. Thus, I created this book to serve as a guide through the early years of your sports career.

Earlier in my career, I experienced some rough patches, and as I graduated from college, I noticed a pattern; many skaters were reaching out to me on social media platforms, particularly Instagram, asking me a couple of very similar questions. This got me wondering how many of such people had the same questions in mind but did not have someone accessible like me and have simply been restricted to learning from avoidable mistakes

The truth is, if I had been exposed to many of the luxuries that would be shared in this book, it would have saved me a lot of stress, anxiety, financial problems, and other mistakes. This is why this book is so important to me. To share with you many of the things I wish I had known before starting this lifelong journey.

One thing I am certain you've heard over and over again is the fact that change is one unavoidable importance in one's life. It is the only constant in this rollercoaster ride called life. And to survive and succeed through its highs and lows, you need to be able to properly navigate the scenarios you encounter on the ride and adapt as you progress. The outcome on any ride is dependent on your level of resilience and will to reach your destination. In other words, all rides are enjoyable, but some are scarier than the next. Thus, the only way to truly enjoy each and every ride is to see beyond that fear and focus on what you hope to achieve on that ride. This could be happiness, freedom, or it could even be a sense of tranquility for others. Find that purpose which resonates with you and stick to it.

The turning point of my career would be that moment when I started to have deep focus and believe in my abilities. Trust me, I know it is not as easy as it may seem but find the people who belong in your corner, those that would support and genuinely drive you. Of course, I had my family, coaches, and a few friends that helped me on this journey, but still, finding the time, energy, and courage to simultaneously practice the violin while figure skating competitively and excelling in college was hard.

It was mostly a difficult situation because of the lack of guidance. I was creating my own format as I progressed. I had no footsteps to follow; no one was interested in the things I was invested in like I was. My life was like a blank canvas; I could paint any way I wanted. I had to ask myself if I wanted to become a Picasso or Michelangelo or if it was possible to draw from both and create my own legacy. As time passed, I learned that every moment I wasted comparing myself to others was simply time wasted on my freedom and happiness.

The main aim is to assist you in functioning at your highest potential while you pursue your goals and attain success. If I were to analyze my life from the beginning until now, I would be proud of myself for achieving what I have so far. This is exactly how I want you all to feel. Life is like a flower - you have to water it and give it sunlight to grow. I hope to help you grow your flower, too.

Whether you are pursuing sports, hobbies, music, crafts, or anything else, I hope to guide you towards balance as you learn to merge your passions with your academic life as a student.

I will share insights into mental health, anxiety issues, time management, purpose, passion, vision, income, confidence, happiness, organizational skills, efficiency, drive, and more - all the things I had to learn the hard way. All useful information and insights that you can apply in your life. We all know how it feels to learn through trial and error. But, while we grow from our mistakes, it's not an easy way to learn. This book will help you choose the best path for you when pursuing sports and extracurricular activities in college. Then, with diligent commitment, focus, and discipline, you can achieve your goals.

*"Live as if you were
to die tomorrow.
Learn as if you were to
live forever."-GANDHI*

Chapter 1

About Me

In 2020, I graduated college as a pre-medicine student while

simultaneously competing as a national and international figure skater

for Norway, competing for LVFSC in the United States, and Training

with LA Elite Ice, but my journey did not follow the traditional four-

year college experience that you are most likely familiar with.

Going into college, I had dreams, hopes, and excitement as any other

fresh high schooler. I was already so much invested in figure skating.

In fact, some would say I was passionate about it. I had an idea that a

focus on sports might be in the future for me, but I also understood the

need for good education.

So, I embarked on a journey that parallels each other and would require

two seemingly different individuals. I embarked on a journey as a

student-athlete, but I had no idea what it would take to stay healthy in

body, mind, and spirit. Since I knew that I would never give up figure

skating, I planned to graduate with a biology degree in three years

while competing as a senior figure skater. This required me to reserve

three hours every day to practice, plus one hour for transportation to

and from the ice rink. This equaled four hours towards my training per

day, all while staying consistent in my studies. In addition, I needed to get good grades in school to keep my academic scholarship at UNLV while maintaining my athleticism and competitive edge.

You would expect everything to go rather smoothly since I knew what I was getting myself into from the start, right? Well, this is not always the case, especially for me, as I was in for a rude awakening during my sophomore year of college.

But then, it all seemed perfect; I was in college for a degree, maintaining a social life and pursuing my passion as a figure skater. I thought I had created a balance until this lifestyle started to take its toll on me.

I became sleepless. I couldn't have a functioning public activity on the off chance that I needed to get passing marks. I needed to forfeit one piece of my life for another. I didn't possess energy for things I delighted in, like exercise, cardio, and doing my top pick on-ice and off-ice preparing. My inclinations were being compromised, some of which were crucial for my prosperity as an Olympic skater. I didn't have as much energy on the ice as I was utilized to. I was not proceeding also practically speaking. I didn't understand what these trade-offs were meaning for my life adversely. Change can be frightening, and as opposed to excusing signs from God or the universe so you can turn into your best self, you need to acknowledge that what worked once is done working.

The time had come to collect another method of getting things done; my longing for progress remained, yet rather than fixating on the little subtleties of my life, I turned out to be more vocal about my battles and looked for help.

In high school, when I was investigating colleges and talking with my advisor, I didn't comprehend that it was fundamental for me to pick a school with a skating program, or if nothing else, a school that helped sports and scholastics. I learned through experience that a school like that may have profited me more. However, I made the best of my circumstance. I went to UNLV because the stunning Surya and Suzanne Bonaly were training in Las Vegas at that point, and I got an academic grant to go there. However, these may have been valid justifications as life unfurled, my choice wound up misfiring on me, and I'll clarify how all through the book.

I started to understand that being a university student competitor is undeniably more troublesome than being an ordinary student. In addition to the fact that you are turning into a full-time student and assuming school life obligations, you are also assuming the duties and assumptions for a full-time competitor. You need to remember numerous components before choosing to progress forward with sports and different interests like workmanship, music, composing, and that's just the beginning while in school.

As often as possible, I felt a void in my journey through college since I was an international student. English is my fourth language, and I didn't identify with the American culture from the outset. Be that as it may, the fortunes that were my experiences made everything great.

On the off chance that you are an international student or an individual that has left your home to study or pursue your dreams consistently be receptive to new things and circumstances since probably the best achievements and recollections are made out of your usual range of familiarity. You need to recollect what motivates you. Ask yourself: what is your "why?" Why did you pick this path?

Each time I recalled the sacrifices my mom made for me to have the option to figure skate and how I had such enormous dreams as a young lady, it consequently refueled me. On the off chance that you need to add a spark to your life, moving away from your home or taking a gap year from your nationality will offer you a chance to learn alternate points of view and develop your profound knowledge. I didn't let the dread of the obscure prevent me from pursuing my dreams in any event when I was frightened. Today I can say I wouldn't have done it some other way.

Focus equivalents power. On my journey to succeed, I figured out how to be amazing, vunlerable, and beautiful. However, I battled to settle on choices with my brain over my heart. Finally, I understood that your hunch never bombs you, and that is the voice that will direct you through life.

If you are a international student, know this, I am excited for you to set out on your journey. However, studying in an alternate nation will expect you to adjust to new circumstances, and you will adapt to a lot, such as, as new dialects and new societies.

As an international student, you are only privileged to have certain jobs on campus. My sessions on the ice were toward the beginning of the day. I had a nearby jobn in HR, and I worked at the reception in my junior year. This depleted my energy. Eventually, I couldn't oversee anything.

Sooner or later, I understood the college in Las Vegas was not supporting my skating, yet at first, I needed to skate with my mentors, Surya and Suzanne Bonaly. Surya was my motivation since I was a young lady. Preparing with her reignited my enthusiasm. I was more resolved than any other time in recent memory to arrive at my objective of turning into a senior public Olympic skater. Surya was frequently a disputable skater; she set out to do what nobody else could; she landed reverse somersaults on one foot at the world and Olympic titles, notwithstanding it being unlawful. Having her as my mentor was a once in a blue moon opportunity that I will always remember. She is additionally a dynamic individual. I was happy that I had the chance to skate with her.

My mentors instructed me that life outside of skating will be intense; however, all the difficult work that I put into skating would ultimately help me become more grounded throughout everyday life.

"When you fall, you get back up; this builds character."

- Suzanne Bonaly.

My years skating instructed me that disappointments will occur, however regardless of how things turn out, badly or not, you need to get back up and attempt once more. Nonetheless, I encountered an especially difficult situation when Surya moved to Minnesota during my first year. After she left, I understood I was at the wrong school. There were relatively few assets accessible for me there for preparing, and Surya had moved away. I continued battling this inclination and revealed to myself that it would be okay. My grant at UNLV was keeping me away from leaving even though I knew the best thing for me was to move to California and get another mentor. I was anxious to get my certification and graduate. Money isn't everything over the long haul; the only important thing is the thing that you get from your encounters and how those encounters shape your character.

I at last settled on the decision to move to California and move colleges in 2017. When I changed schools, I understood I ought to have settled on the choice before. As the days passed, my transition to California ended up being an insightful choice. I began improving at skating and got an opportunity to skate with Derrick Delmore and Peter Kongkasem, Angela Nikodinov, and Sia. It abandons any uncertainty that preparation with the group at LAeliteice was probably the best thing that had at any point happened to me. In spite of the fact that I wrongly went to Las Vegas, changed colleges in my scholastic profession, and was held back in school by two years, I actually feel content with my choice today.

My recommendation to any individual who has gone to some unacceptable college and acknowledged it will be: it's never past the point where it is possible to follow your fantasy. Pay attention to what your heart is outlining for you, ask about it, and continue onward. For my situation, I squandered the cash I thought I was saving through my grant at UNLV because I wound up burning through two additional years in school.

I need to give schooling equivalent significance to the enthusiasm for my game. Without instruction, we would not comprehend the little particles that we as people are comprised of as far as possible up to the unfathomably enormous designs through which we exist. Instruction is the structure square of our profession; it's anything but a spine.

On the off chance that you are resolved to follow your energy and overlook your investigations, I request that you reevaluate your needs in light of the fact that there is space for both. Attending a university shows you structure and basic reasoning abilities that are very helpful.

Consider it a reinforcement plan. On the off chance that you end up

with energy for singing, yet might want to seek after designing, you

can, in any case, follow your dreams while finishing a degree in

designing.

If you figure out how to keep a good arrangement between the two,

nobody can prevent you from being effective.

You need Self-discipline to reach Success
"A man who dares to waste one hour of time has not discovered the value of life."
- Charles Darwin

Chapter 2

Time Management

"Time is free but it's priceless, you can't own it but you can use it. You can't keep it but you can spend it. Once you've lost it, you can never get it back." - Harvey Mckay

Is it just me, or is time a social construct? When I was on time for my first event of the day I managed to be on time for everything else throughout the rest of my day and if I was late, the domino effect continued. I found it difficult to stay in the moment because my schedule was packed from dusk till dawn, and with additional distractions such as social media, my anxiety started to build.

I later realized that "all you need are these: certainty of judgment in the present moment; action for the common good in the present moment; and an attitude of gratitude in the present moment for anything that comes your way." —MARCUS AURELIUS, MEDITATIONS, 9.6

In sophomore and junior year of college, I had many sleepless nights and had a lot on my plate. Every Monday and Wednesday I had biology and chemistry labs along with separate lecture classes three times a week, as well as homework and figure skating practice 6 times a week.

When I moved from Norway to Las Vegas and Los Angeles, one of the biggest shocks I experienced was the number of homeless people around campus and around the town. Once I noticed this I knew I had to help, so I became an active volunteer at a homeless shelter for women and a separate shelter for veterans in Las Vegas. I also volunteered at the children's hospital for cancer and hemophilia twice a week for volunteer hours within the field of medicine, and on top of that, I was working at HR at UNLV. My schedule was packed. Even during the summer, I enrolled in multiple classes. I thought this would help me graduate from my 4-year program within 3 years so I could take a gap year and focus on skating. I was gravely mistaken. Because I tried to rush the process, a series of unfortunate events unfolded which set me back on my journey. I also made some poor decisions. What I learned is: you will never be one hundred percent certain of everything you do, but you have to believe in yourself and what you are doing.

When things go wrong do not waste too much time dwelling on the past. You have to keep moving, your assignments still need to be turned in at 12 and no matter how overwhelmed you feel, and you have to go to practice in the morning. Do not complain; make it happen. I know that sounds harsh, but life is hard. When things go wrong, find healthy coping mechanisms that work for you, and use them to brush off your negative thoughts and keep pushing.

The people you surround yourself with and spend your time with can either break you or make you; always remember that your energy and time are priceless. If the wrong people drain your energy or put you in a bad space, you need to recharge. That is time you could have spent on bettering yourself. Your friends can determine your future.

Even if you love someone, if they get you in trouble or don't value your dreams, the relationship will not serve your bigger purpose in life and you have to cut them off. Your time is priceless. If you spend time with people that are highly ambitious then you will become ambitious because "birds of the same feather flock together." You have to let go of things that are not serving you, so you can make space for things that do.

"When you are distressed by any external thing, it's not the thing itself that troubles you, but only your judgment of it. And you can wipe this out at a moment's notice "-- MARCUS AURELIUS, MEDITATIONS, 8.47

Forgive my exaggeration, but if I got a penny every time I told someone about my busy schedule and they responded, "You must have such good time management skills," I would be a millionaire by now. It surprised me to hear that, because my weakest skill set was time management. But respectfully and understandably, with a schedule like mine, one would assume that my time management skills were impeccable. They were not. So, how did I manage to accomplish everything? I have worked so hard to understand the concept of time and the philosophy behind it, and find that it is best summarized:

"A man who dares to waste one hour of time has not discovered the value of life." - Charles Darwin

Mastering time management is a healthy habit to develop. How you organize your time determines the outcome of your day. Time management makes your life easier, as you can add multiple tasks in a single day and get the maximum benefit from each of them. I practiced improving my time management during my senior year of college. It made a huge difference when it came to finishing assignments and having time to rest afterward.

Here are some useful methods for time management:

#1 The Ivy Lee Method

You write down 6 tasks from the most important to the least important and do not move on to the next task until the first one is completely done. Move leftover tasks to the next day.

#2 The Pareto Principle

This is an 80:20 ratio of cause and effect. Pareto's principle predicts that 80 percent of effects derive from 20 percent of causes. This means that if you input twenty percent of work you will receive eighty percent of the outcome.

#3 Use a Google sheet and make a 25-year vision/plan, including things such as health, career, goals, and relationships. Then include a five-year goal, one-year goal, and monthly milestones.

#4 Google Keep a to-do list. This feature works for Androids and Apple devices, and you can use it to make lists and check off tasks quickly. It gives a sense of accomplishment and structure.

Time management is crucial not only for balancing your studies and social life but also for your health. Partying all weekend long, staying up all night, and then having to prepare for assignments is a very hard way to make it through college. I do agree that we as students are always looking for ways to alleviate some of the hectic college routines and have fun with our friends – this is why we tend to mismanage our time.

When managing your time, incorporate rest days for yourself. It is essential in order for your muscles to rebuild and repair themselves, which will allow you to gain even more strength. I messed up because I tried to push it to the limit with lack of sleep, an extreme training schedule, and high-level science courses at UNLV. Had I incorporated resting time in my schedule I would have thrived, and once I did my life got so much better.

"Our rational nature moves freely forward in its impressions when it:

1) Accepts nothing false or uncertain;

2) Directs its impulses only to acts of the common good;

3) Limits its desires and aversions only to what's in its power

4) Embraces everything nature assigns it."

-Marcus AURELIUS, MEDITATIONS, 8.7

During college, I used to take Sundays off to regroup. The tricky thing about being a student-athlete is that if you take a day off from training, you end up studying for an exam, quiz, or just reading for homework. You have to remember that you may have given your body rest, but your brain is still working and that can still make your body tired. I personally always studied at least a little bit on Sundays because I had quizzes due. However, I tried to use it as a day to relax. I would clean my dorm room and then go get food with friends. By Monday, I would feel like a brand new person ready to take on the week.

On weekends I had tournaments or competitions, things became way more hectic and I didn't get my rest day. That's why during the off-season it is essential to prioritize rest at least one day a week. It will make your body and mind stronger and allow you to unwind. If you are able to take a day off from social media on your rest day as well, I highly recommend doing so.

For any student-athlete, it is important to create a routine each semester; layout which days you will cook or buy food, factor in rest and sleep, homework, part-time jobs, and any other responsibilities you have. Dedicating a certain part of your day to specific tasks will make your life much easier. You will be able to achieve as much as possible within your capacity for the day without overworking yourself.

Arrange all the activities of your day according to their priority. Finish the task that is your highest priority first so that you have plenty of time left to finish the other work instead of rushing from one task to another. My main goal to teach you about time management is that you can pay attention to your needs as well. Yes, I know that goals are important in our lives but don't let them compromise your health. You need to make sure that you are going to bed at the right time and getting enough sleep. Sadly, student life is very busy, and we sometimes don't take care of our health the way we should.

Time management will not only help you in staying healthy, but you will soon be able to see that you have become punctual in your life and that is what's required of a professional. Always have a journal by your side in which you have written all the important tasks you have to accomplish that day. Don't make the mistake of overwhelming yourself with what's going on in your life. There will be days when you feel like procrastinating. It is normal. In those moments we have to reflect on what our goal is, and why we pursue it. You can turn procrastination into hard work if you understand why you are doing the work in the first place. Instead of procrastinating, once you finish your tasks, relax, breathe, and turn your devices off even if it's for a short period of time. Regroup and recharge.

I was the girl who used to get A's all of my freshman year, but when junior year hit, my GPA started to decline. I soon realized that being overwhelmed by so many things at once and not being able to manage my time properly was getting in the way of my success and peace of mind. I decided to create a better routine for myself. In this routine, I made sure that I was not throwing myself under a lot of pressure. Soon, I started seeing an improvement in my life and my daily routine.

There are many time management skills that you need to master if you want to avoid stress and be productive. Keep in mind that important tasks matter and you need to make time for them as soon as you can because otherwise, they can have serious consequences for you and others. Once you are done with the most important tasks you can move on to the least important. By the end of the day, you will feel more at ease.

Your Health Should Depend on Your Habits and Nutrition, Not on Medicine

Chapter 3

Health and Nutrition

Who are you, and what does your body mean to you? We often answer

this question with a surface-level answer. Because we are chasing so

many things in life, we never take the time to explore what our body

means to us. I promise you that you will have a much easier time

finding the right foods to fuel your body type if you can consciously

answer those questions.

Maintaining a healthy diet is hard for everyone, but when you move

away to college it can become an even bigger challenge. When I moved

into my college dorm room, the first thing I noticed was that there was

no fridge or kitchen. I was used to cooking at home. In the morning I

would eat cereal or oatmeal and bring a banana, pear, and granola bar

with me to the rink. For lunch, I either went back home and made rice

or salad and added my protein of choice. At the time I was vegan, so

my choice of protein was usually tofu or beans.

My dinner often varied but I ate a lot of quinoa, a different choice of

protein and kale or spinach salad, as well as a cookie or other dessert

since I have a sweet tooth. As you can imagine, when I moved into the dorm and had no kitchen, microwave, or fridge my diet changed - not because I wanted it to but simply because I had to conform to the new environment I was in. Most schools have a student union, and at UNLV it was a huge place where all the students went to get food. They provided a good variety, and everyone that lived in the dorm got a meal plan and a certain amount of available funds to use toward food each semester. The Student Union had Starbucks, Panda Express, Metro Pizza, Subway, Greens To Go, Taco Bell, and my favorite at the time, Jamba Juice. With the meal plan, it is highly necessary to budget, because eating at all of these places 3 times a day adds up quickly and you need the money to last for almost 5 months. We also had a dining common, which was a separate entity from the student union. The setup resembled that of a buffet. We were able to swipe our meal cards there (I believe we had 120 swipes per semester).

The food I was eating was not bad, but it was not what I was used to eating and since eating out every single day as a high-level athlete is not beneficial, I gained 15 pounds my freshman year - aka the "freshman 15." To avoid ending up in a similar situation, I advise you to get a mini-fridge and microwave in your dorm room if possible. I know it's not the cheapest item to buy, so you can email your roommate before school starts and ask what their budget is and if they would like to split the cost with you on a mini-fridge and microwave. Walmart and Target have some really nice and affordable college essentials.

I know that some college buildings have a kitchen, which would alleviate a lot of stress from your diet and allow you to continue to cook and eat similarly to how you did at home. However, if you don't have that option, you have to work with what you've got, but remember that as an athlete your health is of utmost importance, therefore, planning out your diet is critical. It is essential to eat at least 3 meals a day. If you eat at consistent times every day, especially Monday through Friday, you will feel so much more energized. Setting an alarm to eat a snack is really helpful if you are super busy, that way you are reminded to eat. Always keep in mind that food is fuel for your body, just like a car needs gas in order to run.

Diet is an essential building block for your life, and creating structure and healthy habits around food can make your life so much easier. If you don't, you risk burning yourself out. There are many substitutes for unhealthy foods such as replacing candy with fruits, fried foods with non-fried foods, and milk chocolate (as a Norwegian I will admit that melkesjokolade is my favorite thing) with dark chocolate. If you like to eat fruits but don't have access to buy any, drinking a smoothie can replace some of those nutrients.

Ordering a smoothie without artificial flavoring is best in my opinion, but smoothies can be solid sources of Vitamin C and Vitamin D, and along with a great amount of fiber can help you get the nutrients you are missing. Approximately 95% of Americans do not meet the recommended daily fiber intake. Some fruits contain insoluble fiber that your body is unable to break down with digestive enzymes, which cleanses your body by flushing harmful carcinogens out and maintains a healthier and cleaner digestive system (https://www.healthline.com/nutrition/22-high-fiber-foods). There is a plethora of options to choose from, and always keep in mind things that work for another body may not work for yours, so it is an experiment.

Taking advice from other healthy people has always helped lead me on the right track, and then I would just alter the diet as I went along. I don't recommend going on any crazy diets - "lose weight quick" is so stressful - I know from experience. I have a very slow metabolism, but always wanted to lose weight fast for skating. It is essential for me to stay at a certain weight especially during competition season, however, once I was able to settle into a routine and listen to my body, I saw results. Drinking a large amount of water, and going to bed before midnight made a huge difference for me, though as a college student I stayed up late a lot of nights. The nights that I went to bed early made such a significant difference for me. Finding balance is essential, which I discovered over the summer of freshman year when I was living at my Godmother's house. I went on the "Lemonade diet" while she was away for vacation (I know most people probably would have thrown a party instead of opting for the Lemonade diet!). I discovered this diet when I was reading a non-health-related blog post on USA Today. They wrote that Beyonće did it all the time and this was one of her go-to methods of losing weight, and let me tell you, I was flabbergasted.

The moment I read the line about her losing 20 pounds, I was already on my way out the door. I booked it to my car and before you knew it I was at the grocery store looking for the ingredients: Cayenne pepper, lemons, maple syrup, and water. On the recipe and in the instructions it said to start slowly and only drink this liquid for 2 weeks. I was so eager to lose 10 pounds quickly I did not consult with a medical doctor before trying this which is very dangerous. One thing I will note is that I started on a Friday and I did not have practice during the days when I went on this diet, as I believe it would have been impossible to be on the Lemonade diet and train at a high level. I ended up feeling nauseous the first couple of days - the taste was unsatisfying and I felt hungry.

I barely lasted 4 days until I had to eat something solid. At 20 years old and with the amount of serious training I was doing it really was not necessary for me to go on such a diet, but the pressure from figure skating to always be thin was on my subconscious mind. I like to believe that I had everything under control but at times I was overwhelmed and felt the need to lose excessive amounts of weight quickly. If you have such thoughts I recommend getting a therapist because it can help you ease a lot of stress from your life.

Looking back at this now, I could never even imagine doing something like that. Beyonće is a celebrity with access to nutritionists that most people do not have, including me. USA Today is not a peer-reviewed scientific nor scholarly site thus the information written has not been verified by experts. As I progressed through college I read numerous amounts of scholarly articles and learned the importance of doing proper research and gathering information from peer-reviewed articles, which allows you to make the best choice for what suits you. So if you ever decide to go on a diet please be careful and make sure to complete all necessary research. While I do not recommend going on any diets, I do recommend having a consistently healthy diet, as this is the building block for creating healthy habits and will help you accumulate a rich life. Never forget that Health is Wealth.

 Have you ever thought about the nutrients, minerals, and essential vitamins that we are unable to get through unhealthy eating? Let me ask you: when was the last time you had an apple for an evening snack? Or the last time you blended up a scrumptious (but healthy) banana smoothie with some berries for breakfast? Have you thought about managing your diet in a way that allows you to get all your important nutrients throughout the day? These nutrients include vitamin C, vitamin D, protein, iron, and so on. Again, I know that college life is very exciting as you just want to have a good time with your friends but keep in mind the other aspect of college as well. Don't forget the sleepless nights when you are occupied with tasks like doing your homework, submitting that assignment, or passing that test. There is also training that you have to attend and although your coach may already be giving you similar advice, to remain fit in any sport you need to make sure that you are strong internally.

Our physical appearance can often deceive us. You may feel happy to see your skin glowing, your body in the perfect form, and your workout timings accurate. But I would recommend you take care of your body internally as well, as how well our internal components are working is also a measure of health.

The most important nutrient you must include in your diet to maintain your health is water. If you are eating all the right nutrients but still feel dehydrated, check the last time you finished two bottles of water throughout the day. There are lots of benefits when it comes to drinking water. These benefits include:

•Improved mood and memory

•Reduced sugar cravings and help in the maintenance of a healthy weight

•Improved workout performance

•Reduced incidences of migraines or headaches that you may have occasionally due to stress or bad lifestyle choices.

•Improved digestion and reduced constipation

•Prevent kidney stones as it dilutes the substances from being able to develop the stones

•Reduced chances of getting a bladder infection

•Helps you stay hydrated after drinking alcohol (I know that college is another name for hangovers. So drink your water!)

You may be aware that experts suggest drinking at least 8 glasses of water throughout the day. Be very mindful when it comes to adding syrups to your water because that will increase your sugar intake and can do more harm than good. You can drink detox water instead. You can make this at home by using fruits and vegetables. I like to add slices of strawberries or cucumbers. It is a healthy alternative and will help you stay fresh and active throughout the day while detoxifying your body.

You can also add orange juice, eggs, chicken, nuts, fresh fruits, and vegetables to your diet and avoid junk food as much as possible. If you are vegan or vegetarian then lentils, beans, and legumes with protein are essential for your protein intake. I am telling you this because I want you to be fully prepared when it comes to maintaining a healthy diet in college.

If you are a foodie and saying goodbye to junk food sounds like a nightmare to you, then I have got you as well. Follow a strict diet throughout the week fulfilling all the nutrients that your body needs and it will thank you later. Once you have managed to do that successfully, you can spare one day of the week to reward yourself for your dedication and patience! This way all your cravings will be satisfied and you will feel content and motivated to keep going with your healthy diet. If you love sweets or crazy about junk food then you are familiar with the term "cravings." Yes, they happen, but I want to let you know that it's okay to have unhealthy food cravings now and then. My suggestion to you is to not resist yourself when you are craving something. This will only give more power to the craving and by the end, you will be so drained of controlling yourself that you will eventually give up on your healthy eating plan and consume all the junk food available to you.

If you follow my tips and satisfy your cravings you will find that you can remain motivated to follow the healthy diet plan, as you will not be feeling the urge to eat something unhealthy all the time. By doing this, you will be telling your body that you can have that particular food you love so much at any time of the day. It is totally under your control, but you just don't choose to have it right away. Thinking this to yourself will send a positive signal to your brain and your cravings will eventually be reduced as you get used to your new healthy diet with each passing day.

I am going to tell you a story to help you understand the importance of maintaining your health. I spread myself so thin and didn't realize it was taking a toll on my health. I was diagnosed with hypotension due to hot weather, dehydration, and the pressure of getting all things done and having so much work to do. During my junior year, my biology teacher was offering extra credit in his class if students donated blood on campus during finals week. I was thrilled because I could help someone and I knew that the final could bump my grade up to a B+. When I went to donate blood the nurse had a hard time finding my blood pressure. She tied a band around my arm. She took that off and tried to check my pulse and still nothing. She went to her colleague and I saw them whispering. She returned and tried again, then asked if I felt okay. I said yes, and she said "your blood pressure is extremely low, 84/40mmHg." In my defense, I am an athlete, and people that train a lot usually have slower heartbeats. However, she advised I see a medical doctor immediately because regular blood pressure is 120/80mmHg. I begged her to still draw my blood because I really needed that extra credit for my biology class, but she looked at me sternly and said "we can't draw your blood."

In retrospect, I'm glad she didn't. I can't even imagine what would have happened if I had not gone to donate blood that day. I thought since I ate healthily and I still felt okay despite the extreme fatigue and lack of sleep I had, that my health was fine. I also had to acclimate to the dehydration that comes with living in the desert, as a Norwegian moving to Las Vegas. After this incident, I started taking my health seriously and began to drink Powerade along with lots of water to keep myself hydrated throughout the day. So make sure you stay hydrated - drink lots of water!

As I mentioned above, the weather in Las Vegas impacted my health more than I thought it would. My hair and skin felt dry, and I became dehydrated which I was not used to. If you move to a cold climate from a hot climate I definitely recommend doing research about that before you move. For example, if you relocate to a place that has a lot of snow, make sure that you have enough blankets, hats, gloves, scarves, a heating pad if necessary, and a portable heater. I know it may seem like common sense but sometimes when we move it's easy to forget essential things and before you know it, you are shivering in a blizzard only wearing a small jacket and shorts, wondering why you chose that school.

Living in Las Vegas was such a wake-up call for me because the 102 degree heat on a good day was just not something I was used to. I had to visit a cardiologist because I was getting heart palpitations, which was concerning as I had already gone through heart surgery when I was younger. Your academics are important, grades are important, passion is important, but you must always keep your health in mind. You cannot accomplish your goals if you don't have your health.

To this day I don't drink alcohol because of my heart condition nor do I smoke anything, but I still had to go through so many health problems simply because I was not doing the same things that I used to do before college to maintain my health.

It is important to prepare your mind and body before going to college so you don't get hit by the sudden change in routine in a negative way. I'm not saying that college is a place completely cut off from the world or on a remote island, but managing college academics with sports is an art and to master this art you must take care of your body internally and externally. What can we do to fix our bodies internally? There is no "normal" way to do this; a spider will weave a web expeditiously and feel comfortable in the process, while a fly will buzz by and experience chaos and trauma in that same web. Do not be discouraged if you don't see results right away or if a certain workout or diet worked for your friend but not for you. Consequently, if you approach your goal with a good attitude and the necessary research the journey will be more satisfying and fulfilling and it won't feel as bleak while you try to collect the tools you need to fix and maintain your internal and mental health.

I remember when I kept falling and falling on my triple toe I was so frustrated in tears because it was consistent and before the competition I had lost it, my coach Suzanne told me that it builds character. Snow and ice all the way up my leg, I brushed the tears off my face with my ice-cold hands as my gloves had been soaked from the snow remaining on my gloves from the falls. At that moment, I remember thinking "oh whatever, I just want to land my triple toe," but that moment has replayed in my head several times during 2020. The character that I have built through years of not giving up, learning work ethic, and most of all getting back up when things seem impossible despite being in pain are the building blocks to my life. I say this because I want you to understand that failure doesn't always mean that you failed. You can learn to view failure as a lesson when you try to guide yourself and your human ever-changing body (especially as women, our bodies change all the time). Finding a new balanced diet might fail so many times, however, every time you fail you learn a lesson, and when you do I want you to write it down in your notebook or diary because, in the end, you will have the recipe you need for success.

The goal is to find a diet that feeds you internally, mentally, and allows you to be healthy at the same time. If you are someone who struggles with this I want you to know that you are not alone; it took me years to balance everything and each year I feel like my body reacts differently to certain things that I used to enjoy. I used to eat cereal almost every morning, but now it makes my stomach hurt. Now I enjoy eating fries and before I didn't; the glass is always half full no matter what angle you choose to look at it from. The choice is yours.

Discuss with your coaches if you are having a hard time with your diet or with your mental health. Especially if you have tried on your own, it is important to consult with the people around you or reach out for help. It is best to follow your trainer's instructions so that you can maintain a healthy diet successfully while taking care of your mind, body, and soul. Taking these measures may sound challenging, but your body will thank you in the future. You will soon see a glow in your skin, your body will tone up, your weaknesses will turn into strengths, and your eyes will be sparkling. Trust me when I say once you start following a healthy diet plan and experience the positive change in your life, and feel the balance it creates, you will be so glad you did. Following a healthy and balanced diet to achieve maximum benefit and productivity both in studies and in training will prove to be

very fruitful for you in the long run.

"Your Present Circumstances don't determine where you can go; they merely determine where you start." - Nido Qubein

Chapter 4

Mental Health

"You have been formed of three parts - body, breath, and mind. Of these, the first two are yours insofar as they are only in your care. The third alone is yours truly." - Marcus Aurelius Meditations, 12.3

Anything can happen to our bodies; we can get cancer or coronavirus, our breath can vanish simply because our time here has finished. However, the mind is yours - you own it, and you choose how to treat it. It is your most powerful tool. Your breath and body are also important, but you need to strengthen and protect your mind.

Mental health is a very broad topic. I am not a professional in this matter. However, I will do my best to share the research I've conducted along with what I learned from my therapist. We have to understand the essence of being human to understand the way we think, feel and behave. This will allow us to change our mental state when we wish to improve our mental health. As human beings, we are given an unimaginable amount of dispositions and characteristics. The events that we encounter throughout our lives have a large effect on our mental health. I grew up competing in a sport from the age of seven in a sport where no one looked like me. I wanted to fit in, be understood, and be a part of the figure skating community. However, the moment I understood that that would never happen was the moment I blossomed into the person I am today: fearless, kind, understanding, loving, beautiful, and powerful. I do not seek validation from my sport. I am here now to bring what I have to the table and that's it, whether other people like it or not.

It was important to have coaches that understood I was not a "normal figure skater" - yes, the obvious "she's black" - but in addition to that, I am 5'7" which is tall for a singles figure skater. "Figure" skating puts a significant amount of pressure on skaters and our bodies. Some skaters struggle with eating disorders, and many know someone who does. In spite of all this, I have continued to skate for 20 years. Why? Because it is my passion. Despite all the negative and heartbreaking experiences I have gone through in my sport, I love it so much. The first thing you have to do is acknowledge that you will experience ups and downs and that's perfectly normal.

The most powerful thing you can do for yourself is to learn how to cope with different situations; what you don't want to do is push difficulties to the side, because before you know it years have gone by and you are stuck with a box storing your trauma, depression, anxiety, and stress, and you've thrown the key away into the middle of the Atlantic Ocean as a coping mechanism. And then you have to unravel everything to find the key and open the box in order to unpack everything and fix it all. Sometimes we may not know that we are depressed, but feel sad for no reason or for every reason. I want to let you know it's completely normal to feel sad, upset, angry, or even really happy.

"Globally, more than 264 million people of all ages suffer from depression,"(https://www.who.int/news-room/fact-sheets/detail/depression) so if you find yourself mentally exhausted or depressed, know that you are not alone. There are many resources for you to get help. Your depression is not a reflection of who you are, just a glimpse of your previous experiences. You are whole, though you may feel broken. Once you validate your truth and use the resources available to you such as on-campus therapy (which is usually free) or talking to your friends who may have experienced similar feelings, one day the sky will be the brightest blue color and you might even feel better than you ever did. But it takes time, and even if you start feeling happier the process is sometimes a roller coaster. In 2019 I had regionals in Salt Lake City, Utah, after the semester I'd started going to therapy. Competing in this particular ice rink is always challenging for me due to the high altitude, but it turned out to be one of my best competitions. At 4,637 feet above sea level, despite running my programs 2-3 times a day at practice before a competition, once I was on the ice at that altitude it was truly an experience of gasping for air in the most graceful way I could.

I could hear my coach Sia's voice yelling, "Don't open mouth while breathing" in her Russian accent, and I hope I made her proud because I was breathing through my nostrils for dear life. My therapist was excellent at helping me understand things about my sport and how I could better utilize my time and planning outside of skating to better my performance on the ice. She was not a sports therapist but the sessions I had with her made a huge difference for me mentally. One of the best things I learned and was able to put in action during the competition was to be in the moment, and not allow negative thoughts such as "I'm at high altitude and I'm going to be super tired" or " I gained 2 pounds, I'm going to fall" to intrude on my mindset.

The most interesting thing I can tell you is that even though you can turn negative thoughts into positive thoughts, your subconscious mind is so powerful that you have to actually believe the words you are saying - if not, that fear of the negative thoughts you have will take over. Life is going to challenge you in many ways outside of your sport - love life, family, friends - but the biggest test is how you handle each situation, and you can only conquer the problem if you master your own mind.

This process can take many years, and I will discuss this more in the chapter about mediation. For my short program at regionals in 2019, I got on the ice after the monitor had called the next skater to the ice. I was in my element. I could hear everything my coach Derrick was saying. I felt prepared - like the feeling of finishing a puzzle, all the pieces were coming together and the feeling was immaculate. During my warm-up, I landed my triple sal and my triple loop combo. My spins felt good and the ice was perfect - not too soft, not too hard - a lush magnificence under my blades. After they called out the scores of the skater before me, they announced my name and I skated into my start position. I had the good kind of butterflies in my stomach and I was ready to kill it. I told myself this is going to be a good program. But out of nowhere, the wrong music turned on and I immediately skated over to the head judge.

I felt a dreary ambivalence in my mind and had so many thoughts

rushing through my head. First of all, my music worked the day before

on the official practice ice, so why were they playing a different song?

Was someone trying to sabotage me, what in the Nancy Kerrigan and

Tonya Harding is this? I felt like it was a bad dream because the perfect

program I had imagined in my mind had been altered before I even

started. I just wanted to make it to sectionals and I wanted to skate a

clean program, but in my mind, it had already gone wrong. At that

moment I remembered that I know what I'm supposed to do and that I

had practiced this program and all these elements a thousand times. I

looked over at my coach because he had my extra CD.

 They found my music really fast - it turned out it was the lady at the

music box that had by mistake played another skater's song. The whole

situation took less than a minute to sort out and fix. I thought to myself

"the show must go on," as Satine did in Moulin Rouge (although I

wasn't dying like she was, hypothetically if I didn't make it to

sectionals I would!). And before I knew it I heard my music -

"Diamonds" by Rihanna. I skated an almost clean program. I was

happy with my performance but felt it could have been better. I ended

up making it to sectionals the next day after the long program and the

happiness and joy that I felt were incredible. Even at the high altitude, I

finished strong because I didn't let negative thoughts overrun my mind.
I focused on the task at hand once the music started and that's what I
want you to do when life gets hard.

When life doesn't go as planned, use it as an opportunity to build your
character; let it bring out the best qualities within. You will have to find
your way through unfamiliar territory. Try not to be hard on yourself,
and allow yourself to be comfortable in uncomfortable situations.
Because society needs us to be resilient, it is a law of necessity
especially if you want to accomplish the impossible. Identify your weak
points and handle them before they get worse. Don't let tough times
define you. Without rain, nothing would grow - be resilient even when
the storm comes. You need it for long-term substantial progress.

Marcus Aurelius speaks highly of the law of nature. You must
remember that the way you view the world is your choice, and how you
use your opportunities will lead you to your goals. When I was younger
I was very shy around people I didn't know, and truthfully I still kind
of am, despite competing all around the world for thousands of people.
I am still shy when I'm outside my comfort zone. If you are shy, I want
you to know that people fake their social skills all the time. A lot of
people are uncomfortable in social situations but they pretend like
everything is fine. As long as you are genuine with what you are doing,

may it be performing, giving a speech, or meeting new people, you will, with time, become more comfortable. *"Pass-through this brief patch of time in harmony with nature, and come to your final resting place gracefully, just as a ripened olive might drop, praising the earth that nourished it and grateful to the tree that gave it growth."* — MARCUS AURELIUS, MEDITATIONS, 4.48.2

The things we do, what we watch, and who we interact with; everything affects our subconscious mind. Sometimes we don't realize how much negativity we feed our minds in one day but if you watch carefully, and only accept good vibes around you, it can drastically change your mental health and help with depression. Sometimes removing toxic people from your life can make a huge change in your attitude and outlook on life. Try to incorporate as much positivity in your life as possible. Life can be difficult and unexpected problems may arise, but when problems go away it still does not guarantee happiness. Most times you will have to put conscious effort into becoming happy again.

In a college environment, an easy way to increase positivity in your life is to make your dorm room as comfortable as possible which will allow your mind to relax. I filled my dorm room with pictures of my family, friends, and celebrities that I admire. I downloaded an app that lets you upload as many pictures as you want, and I ordered 200 photos for an extremely affordable price and it took less than three days to receive all of them in the mail. I hung them up on the huge white brick wall on the side of my tiny wooden bed (I chose bed covers that were hot pink with brown leopard print), and once I was done with that I still felt like something was missing so my amazing, sweet roommate Becky and I drove to Target and I bought some fairy lights to sparkle up the room. Once I made my room a comfortable space, I became more effective.

Life is a huge test, and it's up to us how well we perform on this test. From the first moment we open our eyes, we serve this world with our own unique purpose. We grow up and start realizing the true meaning of life. You start as a carefree child with lots of love. All you do is play, eat, sleep, and explore your new world. But then you start growing up, and you start gaining responsibilities. You go to school and have to deal with tests, homework, assignments, essays, projects, and an entirely new, structured life in which you're expected to perform. This is just the way our ancestors designed life to be for us. We take it one step at a time - one chapter, one mathematical concept, one grade at a time - so we are not overwhelmed with too much knowledge at a very young age. This is just how life works – under a system.

We are the basic parts that make up this system. We may not have authority or control in this system, but keep in mind that we as human beings, as families, as a society, and as a country contribute to it equally. We all have our purpose and our place in this society.

Let me tell you - life is not always going to be easy and you will face many challenges. Problems never end. You might be thinking what a depressing chapter this is – but stay with me and you will soon see what I'm talking about. Indeed, we can never get rid of all of our problems but do not be intimidated by the ups and downs. Remember that the greatest philosophers, scientists, and many athletes have already lived, so you have the best teachers only one Google search away. People who love or play sports for a living are not the only ones with problems. Problems are universal and can affect anyone's life.

One of the best pieces of advice I can give you is not to focus on the problem. Focus on your attitude towards the problem instead. This simple statement changed my life forever. I learned that the problem is not within the problem itself, but how you deal with it in your mind and solve it. I used to think about my problems all the time – what am I going to do when I go to medical school? How will I manage everything? I became depressed, stressed out, and fatigued. The result? My athletic performance started declining and my grades started to fall. I let the unknown scare me and steal the joy from my present moment, rather than trusting the process. Your mind can play games with you. It can make every little problem seem gigantic, and what can you do when that happens? Change your mindset, you have to trust yourself. You have to believe that any problem that comes into your life is only there to teach you a lesson. When you start seeing blessings in every problem that you encounter, your life will start changing and you will feel so much joy and contentment.

"What's left to be prized? This, I think—to limit our action or inaction to only what's in keeping with the needs of our own preparation . . . it's what the exertions of education and teaching are all about—here is the thing to be prized! If you hold this firmly, you'll stop trying to get yourself all the other things. . . . If you don't, you won't be free, self-sufficient, or liberated from passion, but necessarily full of envy, jealousy, and suspicion for any who have the power to take them, and you'll plot against those who do have what you prize. . . . But by having some self-respect for your own mind and prizing it, you will please yourself and be in better harmony with your fellow human beings, and more in tune with the gods—praising everything they have set in order and allotted you." —MARCUS AURELIUS,

MEDITATIONS, 6.16.2b–4a

A relaxed mind will improve your mental health so you can carry out

your daily tasks more effectively. Try to change the environment you

are in from time to time such as going outside for study breaks,

studying in the library, at Starbucks, or in the common area as long as

you can focus and the sound level around does not distract you. If you

feel suffocated in a certain place or living with someone, take care of

your mind, and change locations if you can, even if it's only for a little

while. Self-care and making positive changes will affect your life in a

very positive way and help you see how blessed you are.

Make yourself so strong internally and externally that your calm vibe

transfers through your aura and people start feeling positive energy

radiating from you. It all starts with your mind and only you are in

control of how you see, feel, and react to things that are going on in

your life. I know it's easier said than done but believe me, it just takes

one step at a time. It doesn't have to be all at once. Give yourself

breaks every once in a while and you will soon see your mental health

improving. I always had to remind myself there is a difference between discomfort and pain. Your thoughts, your mind, and your dreams belong to you; the universe is infinite and you can be unlimited.

Eliminate stress by participating in activities that make you feel better; things that you love doing. For me, it was hiking, rollerblading, and playing the violin. Whenever I was stressed, I would do one of those activities to make myself feel better and it worked! I also started seeing a therapist during my junior year of college and it was very helpful. If it wasn't for my therapist, my year would have been pretty bad - that's why I recommend that you reach out to your on-campus health programs. Don't worry about paying extra fees because in most cases they are free of cost, and when you have access to free therapy, you should take advantage of that. If you have social media I recommend only following users that make you happy and inspired, so if your timeline on Instagram, Facebook, TikTok, Twitter, or other apps is filled with posts that leave you feeling mediocre and unhappy with your life, then you are not following the right people.

You should go on an immediate unfollowing spree and search for accounts that will instead inspire, uplift, and fulfill your energy in a positive way. Look at your mental health as a beautiful, sparkly, porcelain glass: you can choose to fill it with the purest Norwegian water, or with toxins. The choice is ultimately yours. You are in control, so why not fill it with good vibrations, happiness, and joy? We each have a unique purpose in life, therefore you have to embody your whole self, and understand and recognize what serves you and what doesn't. Being exposed to the wrong things on a regular daily basis will disconnect you from your true purpose in life. The most beautiful thing you can do for yourself is to not fight your journey, but instead accept it and discover where you belong.

If you are in sports through your school's team, chances are that you have access to the resources and benefits made available for NCAA (National Collegiate Athletic Association) athletes at universities. What I want to share with all of you skaters, students, and people in general who do not belong to a school sports team is that there are many resources you can rely on to be mentally strong and kind to yourself. At the top of my list of tips on fighting stress, I encourage you to try my favorite meditation from John Kabat Zinn. He is an American professor of medicine and a creator of the Stress Reduction Clinic who offers many free videos on how to meditate on YouTube. When I tried his first meditation that was 24 minutes long it was hard for my mind to not wander all over the place, but I was able to refocus every time I caught my mind wandering, which is a skill I learned from my therapist. Do not get mad at yourself - rather embrace your mistake and try again. I could feel the stress releasing from my body. My mind was relaxed and I felt more deeply aware after doing his meditations. I felt like I was able to escape all the noise in my mind and be in the moment.

I understand that doing sports is not easy. At times, you will face tough competition and feel defeated, but that's normal. That's how you learn from your mistakes and make improvements - it's just another way to succeed. You have to train your mind to get back to a calm, stable state as soon as you can after a bad competition. You have to keep going so the demons in your head do not convince you that you cannot reach your goals. You have to be in control of your mind and that, my friend, is how you will succeed.

If you make preparations in advance and train your mind how you want it to respond in any situation, then you will create a warrior from the ashes that were meant to bury you. I valued my education as well, but my main priority was to remain fit in sports both physically and mentally. I transferred universities from UNLV to Vanguard, I moved between states, and I had to adjust. But it wasn't as difficult when I started shifting my mindset. All it takes is time for you to adjust, and then you will see that your environment is not the true master of yourself - you are.

Did you know that athletes at every level are constantly under pressure to remain physically fit? This can result in the neglect of their mental health needs, which can have serious consequences. Athletes who belong to a group or do sports professionally face a unique set of challenges and unexpected circumstances that can make them more vulnerable to anxiety and depression. Sometimes athletes feel so much pressure from being expected to give their best at all times that they start to feel that they can't perform to their best abilities due to the added pressure. I know the pressure is real when you are trying to study and follow your passion for sports at the same time, but do me a favor and be less harsh on yourself. Not every day is going to be a good day and that is okay, just remember that it's temporary. Integrate that consciousness so you don't feel powerless on your bad days - that is how you build resilience.

Nobody's perfect, but people have idealized perfection so much that many have fallen for it and ended their lives quite miserably. In the same way, problems cannot be avoided, perfection can never be achieved. What is perfect in one person's eyes is not in another's. It is not within our capacity to be perfect because God did not create us that way. Everybody makes mistakes - the important thing is to learn from them. Sometimes people chase perfection so obsessively that their mental health declines to a great extent and they have to go to therapy to restore a healthy mindset. So please, keep in mind that you can pursue excellence and your own realistic view of perfection.

If you think that you can solve all your problems by being perfect, try accepting and embracing your imperfections instead. Tell yourself it is okay to have imperfections - to gain weight, to experience mental breakdowns, and to bounce back from it all. And you will bounce back - those situations are only temporary. I always wanted to lose weight because I felt my skating would improve if I did. I was so afraid to gain weight that I avoided lifting at the gym because I was under the impression it would make me heavier. Now, I've started to wonder if I would have skated better if I had increased my lifting workouts, but at the time I was just worried about gaining weight. I also put on pounds very easily so this stressed me out, especially during finals. I always feared that the stress of school would cause me to eat unhealthy foods, which at times it did, so I knew subconsciously right before finals that I would gain weight which caused me more anxiety and stress.

To prevent this kind of negative cyclical thinking, my recommendation is to distract yourself from all the negativity around you and focus on your goal. When you learn to love your imperfections, you will soon start seeing them as your power and this attitude will boost your mental health. You will learn to be thankful and accept the ups and downs in your life and realize that although you can't control everything, you can control your attitude and transform it so that it benefits you instead of bringing you down. I've learned so much from being a competitive figure skater for so many years, and as I continue on this path I hope to constantly evolve and blossom into a better version of my current self. With these tips, you will learn to control your mind and harness its power to overcome everything that stands in your path and how to face every situation with integrity and grace. Be you - your magic is you. You are enough, you are loved, and you are strong.

*The Right Time to Pursue
your Dreams is Now.*

Chapter 5

Purpose/Passion

What is your purpose in life? People are always in the pursuit of more medals, money, success, pleasure, and a good reputation. All of these hold some value, but ultimately something will always be missing. Two thousand three hundred years ago philosopher Aristotle asked these two questions which are relevant even now: "What is the ultimate purpose of human existence?" and "What is the end goal for which we should direct all of our activities?" Eudaimonia - a Greek word that means "happiness" or "human flourishing."

Happiness can be figure skating, winning competitions, skiing, eating your favorite pasta, and going on vacations. But the happiness that Aristotle speaks of is the total and final end goal in one's life. When you watch soccer or American football and your team is winning at halftime, they could still lose the game. Eudaimonia is more than that. Your desires and motivation must align with your purpose because that is the ultimate value of your life.

The Earth itself has a purpose. It is a planet where all species including human beings, animals, plants, and birds live. Its habitat is suitable for all living things. The oceans you see, the deserts, the winds, the sun, the animals, insects, and even the tiniest organisms living on the surface of the ice have a purpose. If it wasn't for honey bees, we wouldn't be alive today, because bees support the growth of flowers, plants, and trees. So if a tiny creature like a honey bee is so crucial for human survival, then you too have a unique purpose in life.

I know how it feels to doubt your purpose. I have been there - that's why I want you to always remember that you have a purpose. Who knows how good and professional you will become on your path - you may become a huge star in the future. You could even change someone's life, or create something entirely new.

When I look back at my experiences, I see many lessons from which I can learn. If it wasn't for figure skating, I would have stayed in Las Vegas and continued with just my education, but there was a deeper purpose. I was able to absorb the concept of gratitude and learned how important it was to admire my blessings. I learned how to live in tough situations and weather. I changed universities in the middle of my academic career and it took its toll on me. I was unable to manage my social life, education, and skating all at the same time. I felt like I was drowning; I forgot what my real purpose was. I was so focused on achieving each small milestone that I lost track of the goal itself. I questioned whether I made the right decision changing universities. At the time, I was clueless. All I knew was I had to keep going. If I gave in to my negative thoughts and lost track of my purpose, I was never going to make it - so that's exactly what I did. I stood up, showed up, and never gave up.

There are seven billion people on this earth, it's magical to think that every person has a different purpose in life and contributes in independent ways. May it be doctors, teachers, engineers, and scientists or artists, athletes, musicians, and creators.

How do you start to make your purpose a reality? Take out your arts and crafts supplies and create an awesome reminder in the form of a vision board hang it up on your wall. Add images, quotes, and words that inspire and motivate you, this way, whenever you feel down, lost or clueless you will see the reminder and get motivated to keep going and working towards your goals. Creating a vision board helped me a lot. I placed it on the wall in front of my bed so the first thing I saw when I woke up was my motivational visual. It helped me kick start my day with full motivation and dedication, as I had my purpose in mind. I would remain charged and energetic throughout the day because of the positive message I saw first thing in the morning. You can also include inspirational affirmations like "don't give up," "you can do it" and so on. Make it your inspirational corner and fill it up with your favorite colors and accessories.

Finding your life's purpose is an art and when you master it, there is nothing that can stop you from reaching your purpose. There are many meditations and exercises that you can do to help your mind focus on exactly what it needs.

Meditation helps you filter your thoughts and narrow them down to draw you closer to your purpose. The same way I realized the purpose of my life to be centered around figure skating and my education, you can, too. Try to expand your positive thoughts, your purpose, and passion from your heart like an elastic that creates a shield around you to protect you from negativity, demotivation, and failures. When you change your mindset and believe that everything happens for a reason, you will soon start to see the purpose of your life.

"A bird sitting on a tree is never afraid of the branch breaking because her trust is not on the branch but on her own wings. Always believe in yourself even when no one else does."-Anonymous

As we grow up, our impressions and the way we view life will change. There is just one thing that remains constant throughout our lives and that is our purpose. Always remember why you started in the first place. When I was a little girl skating outside in Norway and the snow was falling on my face, I loved every moment. The passion I felt in my heart while breathing in that cold air was like no other feeling in this world. I feel at peace when I am on the ice. I feel like I belong and that is what keeps me going into the rink at 7 am every day even when I am exhausted. I wanted to become better and was willing to sacrifice going out, hanging out with friends, and partying in order to pursue my passion. When you feel this strongly about pursuing a path, you have found your purpose.

My mom always baked for my siblings and me when we were younger, and there was a special ingredient she would use to make the best bread. In order to have a successful sports career, there is an essential ingredient you need as well; it can either make or break a competitive athlete. If you have this ingredient in your life, then you can evolve into a seasoned athlete. By now you might have guessed what this ingredient is. Yes, I'm talking about passion. Passion is simple, but the most important ingredient you need in your life if you are planning on becoming a successful student-athlete. Have you noticed when successful athletes talk about their careers, they often mention the word "passion" in their conversations? This is because passion is what drives their minds, bodies, and souls. It helps them reach their goals and stay committed to the path they have chosen for themselves. Passion is one of the most basic ingredients to becoming a successful student-athlete.

That is why it's essential you choose the right sport, art, instrument, and major for you. If you don't feel passion for what you are doing, you have to sit down, look in the mirror and ask yourself, "why am I doing this?" The answer will lead you to your passion. Take special care and be honest with yourself, because nothing is worse than living the wrong life.

Having said that, let me make a distinction between passion and purpose. Passion is something that drives us naturally. We don't even realize we have it until something activates it and we become all about it. Purpose, on the other hand, is something that we have to find. You may have to try lots of different things to find your purpose and in some lucky cases, just one try can lead you to find exactly what you were born to do. From there, passion takes you to the next step of success as you feel motivated after every win and you learn from every defeat. Passion is what makes you feel alive and leads you back to your purpose if you have lost your way.

If you feel like you have become lazy or that somehow your passion has decreased, then watch your favorite sport or performer. It will help remind you of your purpose and your goal. Keep in mind that if you are passionate about sports and becoming a successful student-athlete, your chances of failure will be minimized and you will be able to look beyond the distractions.

Purpose and passion are elements possessed by all successful athletes. These athletes are dedicated to everything they're doing. When you love what you do, a task that feels like a burden to others will be an enjoyable activity for you. This is the reason why passionate athletes are the ones who come to practice early and are the last ones who leave.

Unfortunately, when you are an athlete trying to maintain a balance between education and your sports career, you may go through a phase where passion and purpose are completely lost or become blurred. Some athletes do sports just because their parents insist, or they do it to look good. They are not driven by heart, but rather a desire to please others, which is why they are unable to feel passion for what they are doing. There is nothing wrong with pursuing sports without any passion and purpose, but I believe that it limits athletes from reaching their full potential. Numerous parents and coaches make the mistake of seeing the natural talents of some kids but failing to see that their heart and motivation just don't align. They pressure their student or child into learning a specific sport because they have "seen" them perform well while completely ignoring the fact that their child has no interest in the activity.

In this situation, passion and purpose are lost - what you end up with is an athlete who is forced to be in sport and expected to be good at it. Think about the mental damage that does to someone. Imagine you love cooking, and one day, someone decides that all you will do for the rest of your life is karate. Sounds crazy, doesn't it? If you're not interested in doing something, you will never feel motivated to do it.

True student-athletes immerse themselves in the process of their training. Even if they are practicing on a hot sunny day or in a freezing cold ice rink for more than four hours, they will still look back and be proud of what they achieved through their efforts. That level of dedication comes only when you are passionate about something and love to do it. They see the bigger picture; the other side of training hard day and night because they know one day all of their work will be

worth it.

"I am not made like any of those I have seen. I venture to believe that I am not made like any of those who are in existence. If I am not better, at least I am different."
— **Jean Jacques Rousseau**

Chapter 6

Intercollegiate Resources

I reached out to Sarah Arnold, the Athlete development manager at U.S. Figure Skating, for resources for figure skaters who are transitioning to college. She sent me an overview that I would love to share with you so that you can benefit from it. Before you make a decision make sure to check out these 3-minute presentations offered by universities from around the country, all of which offer skating programs. You can also visit the U.S. Figure Skating website to see many existing opportunities including intercollegiate figure skating, open collegiate synchronized and collegiate synchronized skating along the U.S. Collegiate Championships.

When I started competing and attending university, I began to realize that being a collegiate student-athlete requires far more than being a regular student. Not only are you becoming a full-time student and taking on the responsibilities of college life, but you are also taking on the responsibilities and expectations of a full-time athlete on top of that. There are many factors you have to keep in mind before you decide to continue on with sports and other passions like art, music, writing, and more while in college.

Life seems so easy and effortless when we are in high school. We are used to the normal routine of training, and some of us are even homeschooled. Unaware of the transition we are going to face after finishing high school, we believe that we have everything figured out. I find it unfortunate that some students with a passion for figure skating have no choice but to give up on their dreams because of their college choice, and others feel that they can not continue their passions in life or start new ones.

Many schools have not added figure skating to their roster of school sports. There are not many resources available for figure skaters at these universities. There are over 5,300 universities in the United States and only 75 of those schools offer figure skating programs, and more than 45 synchronized skating teams are representing the colleges. There are numerous competitive college skating opportunities for people who come from different backgrounds in skating. Some of these colleges and universities are:

•Boise State University

•Boston College

•Bowling Green State University

•Brandeis University

For those who want to compete after high school or continue with music or your sport of choice, guidance is required for those who want to skate just for fun or want to feel that cold breeze every morning or every now and then - the ones who love figure skating and are going through that transition phase. I feel like these students should be given more than just an option when it comes to skating. After all, it isn't easy to completely cut off from something you love just because you are moving away to college – to me that sounds unnecessary.

Let me present you with an example of a violinist who has been playing for their whole life. When they go to college, they will not be forced to give up their passion completely. Even if they decide not to move forward with their passion in a competitive way, they are still given the option to play music just for fun or relaxation. When things get super stressful, they can get their violin and start playing. My point is, if musicians are given this comfort and necessity, why aren't figure skaters given the same? Moreover, musicians tend to have more opportunities and options, as they can dual major in music or any other field no matter what university they attend. Did you know that there are around 4,634 institutions in higher education in the United States and out of these, around 1,795 institutions offer degree-granting music programs? There are over 3,763,592 people employed in almost all facets of higher education. I can go on and on when it comes to facts and figures. But my heart breaks when I see that the same is not being done for figure skaters. Instead of overthinking and getting frustrated, think of how far you've come and remove any fear you feel, then find ways to create space for your passion even when there is "no space" for it. This chapter is dedicated to collegiate Figure Skating and provides insights for you so that you can take advantage of all the services available to you.

After all the stressful talk, let's move forward to something that is both necessary and essential. Yes, you guessed right - I'm talking about balancing your training, life, adulthood, diet, and exercise. Figure skating requires your time, attention, and most of all – balance. For this sport, you need to make sure you maintain a healthy balance between all the different areas of your life. This way, you will be able to make the most of your passion.

I spoke with my friend Joonsoo Kim who is a U.S national figure skater and an amazing student-athlete. He is in his sophomore year at UCLA, trains at LA Elite Ice, and is also part of the UCLA skating team. I felt that comparing his experiences to mine at UNLV, a school without a skating program would reveal if my struggles were personal or directly related to the lack of resources at my university. I asked him if it was okay for him to miss class or exams to go to competitions such as regionals and sectionals. He said he informed his professors at the beginning of the semester about his competition schedule because he knew he had a pass to sectionals. He planned the semester accordingly so he could attend sectionals. Joon missed a whole midterm exam but was able to work it out with his professor. I, on the other hand, had the opposite experience at UNLV during my sophomore year. I asked my biology professor if it would be possible for me to retake the exam after returning or before I left, and the answer was no. I even had a letter from USFSA but my professor did not accept it because he said it was not a school sport, therefore he could not approve. I ended up getting a zero on the exam because I went to regionals instead of the exam. I do not regret that choice, but this is an example of how important choosing the right school is. I had a scholarship to UNLV, but I ended up dealing with a lot of stress because my environment did not support my dreams and passions.

Everything can happen and nothing can happen, but you must follow your heart. Joon also said that while UCLA does fund their collegiate skating team, he wishes they had more funding because the cost of traveling, costumes, and training time surpasses the budget they have. If you do decide to attend a university without a skating program, I recommend opening a collegiate program at your school, doing fundraisers, and getting more people involved in skating. Also, the most important thing is to try and find a school and location that you can thrive in. Visit the campus first if you can. If you are an international student or live far away from the university you wish to attend, I recommend checking out how close to the school the grocery store is, how far the ice rink is from the school, whether you will be able to take a bus, or if you will be able to get a car or carpool.

The first couple of months of my freshman year, I did not have a car so I took the bus to Las Vegas Ice Center (LVIC). It was pretty simple - I woke up at 5 am, rollerbladed to the bus stop on campus, and took the bus straight up Flamingo. I skated for 1 hour and then went back to campus. Sometimes I would go in the afternoon. One day the bus was stuck because of an accident and I had to get back to campus for a lab quiz. I started walking down Flamingo towards my school. There was a thrift store on the side of the road, and I stopped inside. There, I found a pair of brand-new rollerblades for $25. Can you believe that I bought those and skated the rest of the way? It was almost 6-7 miles! I will never forget that day. It was fun, tiring and it made me realize that when there is a will, there is a way. This happened 6 years ago, before Uber and Lyft. I suppose nowadays you could just take an Uber or Lyft but regardless, the purpose of me telling you this is that in life unexpected things may happen. Just adjust yourself according to the circumstances as soon as you can and you will soon see a solution.

I remember when I was applying to college. I was so confused about what major I should choose. I knew I wanted a degree that would benefit me in medical school, but within STEM there are many majors to choose from. I recommend doing a lot of research on different majors; explore your interests. You can also ask your college advisor any questions you have. They can help students choose what's best for them. We as students who are just transitioning from high school to college need guidance towards college life. It is not easy to decide on your own. You must have total awareness, facts, and figures when choosing a major because it is a decision that can make or break you. I suggest you relax, take a deep breath, and trust your intuition. It is free to email staff in your department and they are more than happy and willing to help you. Take as much help as you can from your family, friends, and most importantly – professors. Keep in mind that most colleges have organized such services and made them available for students, so do your research and seek help if you need it.

After studying intercollegiate resources and the role of colleges in the governance of intercollegiate athletes like myself, I felt very disappointed and hurt. I came to find that I was not the only one who struggled so much because colleges do not realize that athletics are not just an extracurricular activity for some students. It is about following their dreams and passions and they need proper care and guidance to achieve their goals. I think it's time we recognized that American colleges and universities need to better govern intercollegiate athletics. Although there is a lot of hype about student athletics in the media, the sad truth is that colleges are not putting in a lot of effort to resolve the issue and that's disturbing.

College athletics are in a continuous crisis in this country. Years of discussions and proposals have passed to reform, but the gains that have been achieved are only reasonable. No major positive results have been gained from years of struggling. In my time, there was a lack of resources. Today, I think the situation is improving. Now, students are aware of the things going on in society. They know how to deal with legal matters and take care of everything before moving to college. The awareness granted by social media has made it very easy for student-athletes to stay informed about the latest updates, news, and events going on in sports. Social media is also a great platform we can use to support each other. I have seen various groups and pages where a community of student-athletes is formed and they all support each other's passions, dreams, and desires. They help each other and provide comfort in times of difficulty, giving complete guidance as much as possible. Although social media is a great technology, I wouldn't suggest you rely on it completely.

I stand by one thing, which is for colleges to create intercollegiate resources. The more resources you have as a student-athlete, the higher your chances of succeeding in the sport you love. I have faced a lot of problems and difficulties in my career and most people are surprised how I did it. When my biology professor did not accept my request to retake the exam I was disappointed. I even had the letter from USFSA, but he still denied my request because it was not a "school sport." That was the level of ignorance and lack of support my college gave figure skaters. Just like a diamond under pressure, my experiences shaped me into a better, stronger person and I am thankful for everything.

Going back in history, I realized that athletic programs were incorporated into higher learning institutions for a variety of reasons. Back then it was believed that if students participated in sports, it would help them build a strong character, be a source of entertainment while studying, and generate a positive spirit for the school and the community. However, as time passed, intercollegiate students started facing problems. Athletes were not able to pass certain subjects because of the imbalance between sports and education. This happened because of the lack of intercollegiate resources. I think it's very important for colleges to realize that intercollegiate student-athletes are a real entity and they need to address them with more respect, resources, and guidance.

A student like me who had struggled earlier in college and changed universities managed to keep going with my passion for figure skating. Thankfully, I had family and coaches who helped me get through it all. My positive spirit also helped a lot, but I want to speak up for all the student-athletes who are not able to fight the system and their passion for sports starts to fade away. This happens because they are shown that their academic education is far more important than sports. Although education is a must and should be completed, it doesn't mean that sports should be neglected or pushed aside. I respect the student-athletes who are trying their best to fight the circumstances and looking for resources that could help them.

Have a look at this document full of collegiate skating programs, including estimated costs per season and competitions per year. It features universities and colleges all around the U.S.A. The start and end time is also mentioned for each program so that you can decide which days and times you prefer for your schedule. I extracted this information to help you all and I hope that you will make use of it. My main goal is to help all the student-athletes out there who love their sport and are just looking for some guidance.

The reason why I told you about my experiences with Sarah Arnold and Joonsoo Kim is to set the example that you can always ask for help and advice. Never shy away from it. The people who are going through something similar to you will always be there for you because they know how it feels to be in the dark. They will do their best to guide you and help with everything they can. Moreover, when you talk to new people, it gives you a chance to explore different possibilities you may not have thought of. Make sure that you are doing your best and reaching out to every authentic source of information to help you chase your dreams.

*Nothing is impossible. The word itself says I'm possible. - **Audrey Hepburn***

Chapter 7

Vision / Happiness

"Do not dwell in the past, do not dream of the future, concentrate the mind on the present moment."- Buddha

Happiness comes in many forms. Some people find happiness while reading a book under the shade of a tree on a warm sunny day, while others feel happy dancing to their tune while nobody's watching. Can you define happiness? Happiness is unique to everyone. Living in the past or wondering about the future is not the path to happiness. Instead, it is being grateful and present for every breath. Aim to inhale happiness and exhale positive energy.

We as humans are all flawed. We are visibly flawed and have behaviors like being rude, fighting, or hurting others. We have a habit of being ungrateful even if we are blessed with the best. Is it possible to be genuinely happy? Family members will pass away, your pets will pass away; tragic events will happen, that is the law of the universe and the course of life. How does one find happiness in such heartbreaking times? You have to shift the paradigm of your pain, put it into your art, your willingness to accept the pain and continue with your life. That will lead you to happiness.

"True happiness is to enjoy the present, without anxious dependence upon the future, not to amuse ourselves with either hopes or fears but to rest satisfied with what we have, which is sufficient, for he that is so wants nothing. The greatest blessings of mankind are within us and within our reach. A wise man is content with his lot, whatever it may be, without wishing for what he has not."- Seneca

Some people wonder when they will be blessed with what others have. This behavior is toxic. With that attitude, you will never be content, let alone happy. Happiness is not what some other person on Instagram is wearing, how perfect her body is, or how beautiful she looks in the sunlight. It is not getting jealous of the gifts someone has received from their significant other and thinking that you are not blessed. You know why? Even the most beautiful people may cry themselves to sleep for various unimaginable reasons. If you start comparing yourself to others, you will constantly run the race of life that nobody ever wins. Yes, being on top will make you feel good for a little while, but that feeling will fade away soon after it arrives. Soon you will find yourself chasing after another source of "happiness."

"You are not your body and hairstyle, but your capacity for choosing well. If your choices are beautiful, so too will you be." —EPICTETUS, DISCOURSES, 3.1.39b–40a

If you truly want to be happy, focus on your own goals instead of making someone else your "goals." It is being content with whatever you are blessed with instead of focusing on others, because you never know - they may be feeling the same way about you. They might love your smile, your lifestyle, your friends, or your family. We have to realize that life will not always remain the same for us; happiness will not be a constant. You will encounter some bad days that will disturb your mood and demotivate you, but keep in mind that dark days do not stay forever. Just like the sun sets every evening and rises again after the night, the same goes for life.

"Your mind will take the shape of what you frequently hold in thought, for the human spirit is colored by such impressions." —MARCUS AURELIUS, MEDITATIONS, 5.16

You should only pursue what truly makes you happy. Athletes who are not happy in their sport often see every practice, exercise, and warm-up as a burden. They start neglecting their big-picture goals and give in to laziness, lack of interest, and procrastination. If you have chosen a sport as a career just because your coach or parents have pressured you, you are wasting your precious time and energy.

Think about what would happen if you listen to them now, only to fail later on. The amount of disappointment coming your way will be unimaginable. And it will all be for nothing. You will be happier listening to your instincts instead of fulfilling the wishes of others.

When you know that nobody is forcing you to participate in sports, dance, or school, your energy will increase and you will enjoy your time practicing and competing. You will start interpreting every defeat as an opportunity to learn and grow instead of feeling bad for not being perfect. When you achieve that level of maturity and balance, you learn how to master the art of true happiness. You will start feeling content no matter what befalls you. Life is very unpredictable and those of us who realize that nothing ever remains the same are true warriors and are happy at heart.

All of us have a conversation going on in our heads during practice and events. It is the voice that tells you how tired you are of the intensity, that your legs are screaming for help and that you have had enough. This voice tells you that there is no way you can go on at this pace. You must be surprised at how athletes manage to work so hard and hustle even when they have these voices attacking them in their heads. The thing is, they have mastered the art of fighting these voices and in response, they thrive even more. This is what you have to learn if you are planning on becoming a student-athlete. You have to control your inner voice and prepare yourself mentally for even the most extreme strain. The athletes who have mastered this talent know that they can withstand the toughest situations as they have faced them before, so they are confident to do it again. More importantly, they have learned how to disassociate the physical feedback from their bodies which can be painful, from their positive mind.

We get twenty-four hours a day to create our masterpiece. John Heywood once said, "Rome wasn't built in a day, but they were laying bricks every hour." If you want to reach success, you need a clear vision in mind. Think about the big picture. Where do you see yourself in the next 5 years? Do you see yourself practicing/playing/competing on the international level? You need to have a vision of your future self, envision your day, and start laying your bricks. It can be taxing and frustrating, but to reach your goal, you have to face the hurdles.

Try to see these hurdles as small goals instead of obstacles and set them in order of difficulty so that you can jump from one goal to the next.

I have seen a lot of students struggle in both athletics and education because they are unsure about what they are doing. If you are not happy while training and dedicating hours of your life to your sport or something else in your life, how can you expect to excel in it? If something is bothering you and you are not able to focus on practice and events, we must address the issue as soon as possible instead of just dragging ourselves along and getting poor results.

"First tell yourself what kind of person you want to be, then do what you have to do. For in nearly every pursuit we see this to be the case. Those in athletic pursuit first choose the sport they want, and then do that work." —EPICTETUS, DISCOURSES, 3.23.1–2a

You have to decide if you want to pursue sports as a career and ask yourself whether it will truly make you happy. If yes, then all is well. If you are unsure about continuing with sports in college at a competitive level, I suggest you reconsider choosing sports and prioritize your education.

You can always do sports as a hobby. Don't worry, nobody will shame you if you don't pursue sports as a profession. There are millions of people who participate in sports as a lifestyle and there is much joy in that. Some do it to stay fit and others do it because it is healthy for the body, mind, and spirit. "Physical activity increases the flow of oxygen to your brain. It also increases the number of endorphins, the 'feel-good' chemicals, in your brain. For this reason, it's not surprising that people who are in good physical shape also tend to enjoy a higher level of mental agility."- Healthline. I understand that - when you are at the ice rink, your body moves freely. There is a sense of joy that you cannot find anywhere else. Feeling that cold breeze on your face every morning is priceless, whether you are skating for fun or at a competitive level.

This goes for all sports. Your whole body moves, and your mind is activated. Sports are beautiful. You can always return to your comfort zone, and just one game or practice can boost your mood. That is the power of the connection between sports, body, mind, and soul.

You can live a very happy life as an athlete as it allows you to lead a healthy lifestyle. Instead of eating junk food and sitting on your couch all the time, you start preferring salads and workouts. You get addicted to a healthy lifestyle and that is the key to happiness. When you feel light, happy vibes make their way to your heart and lighten your mood. Doing sports also encourages good communication with your opponents. The training you get to speak to your opponent kindly even if you have lost makes you stronger in everyday life, and you become a happier person who is not bothered by anything people say or do. Cooperation is another key to living a happy life, and playing sports will teach you all about it. When you are playing, you are expected to cooperate with your team. You consider your teammates' points of view and even if they are wrong, you strategically talk to them so that they are not offended and also understand your point of view. Before you know it, you start implementing this practice in real life and that's how you become a tactful, cooperative person. Learning and developing these skills that are useful in everyday life by adding athletics to your routine carries incredible worth.

Although sports serve multiple purposes and carry different meanings for everyone, it is safe to say that participating in an organized sport can bring authentic happiness to you and your team. When we are training, we learn how to rejoice in movement and every challenge. Training long and hard hours and waking up early every morning builds character and enlightens us to our strengths and limitations.

You will see so many changes in your life when you realize the importance of happiness and a clear vision while being an active athlete. We often underestimate the power of happiness, and I don't want you to make the same mistakes that I did. Rejoice in every moment. Celebrate every victory, no matter how big or small.

Everything will be okay,
Know that you are Loved.
You are in control of your
inner peace, not external
events or people.

Chapter 8

Anxiety

At some points in our lives, anxiety takes over and makes us feel numb to everything. I used to get anxiety at competitions, and it kept on increasing with every bad experience. I thought it was the end, that the thoughts in my head telling me I couldn't do it was right and I was wrong. I worried I wasn't capable of becoming a successful figure skater. And on my level as a senior figure skater, I felt so much pressure but in reality, the pressure was in my head. At one competition I was so fixated on the skater before me and what she was doing, instead of visualizing my program. Though my mind only slipped for a few seconds, my coach Derek told me at that moment to stop focusing on how my competitors were skating because it didn't matter - the only thing that mattered was how I did. That is the key to beating anxiety - comparing ourselves to others is poison and halts our growth. If you focus all your thoughts and energy on your personal growth, how much better and closer to your goals would you get?

"Our mind can be a beautiful servant or a dangerous master." At nationals last year in my free skate, my body completely "froze" when I was skating, but why? I'd been doing this for years, shouldn't I have mastered this? I had allowed the emotions of my anxiety to take over, and it physically changed the chemistry of my body. I was so nervous I popped several jumps and I barely remember the performance.

"When you let your attention slide for a bit, don't think you will get back a grip on it whenever you wish—instead, bear in mind that because of today's mistake everything that follows will be necessarily worse. . . . Is it possible to be free from error? Not by any means, but it is possible to be a person always stretching to avoid error. For we must be content to at least escape a few mistakes by never letting our attention slide." —EPICTETUS, DISCOURSES, 4.12.1; 19

Athletes have an advantage in the way their minds function. If you miss practice due to schoolwork, try not to stress, because an athlete's body and mind work simultaneously to rewire brain circuits due to years of practice and repetition. It will not be possible to train how you used to in high school when you go to college. You need to remember that you can rely on your body and mind. So don't create extra stress by worrying when you miss a practice due to academics.

Maintaining a healthy balance between sports, academic, and social life is not easy. Your mind is in multiple places at one time. Sometimes you may feel that your mind has frozen and you do not have any energy to go through the struggle. Thankfully my mom was very supportive and she helped me as much as she could, but as she lives in Norway, she wasn't aware of the American system for skating and school also worked differently in Europe. Apart from my mom, I couldn't rely on anyone but myself.

"No one saves us but ourselves. No one can and no one may. We ourselves must walk the path."- Buddha

Seeking help and taking advantage of our resources is essential, but it's up to us to use those resources. To do so can require patience, understanding, and bravery. I was alone in California and had to fight by myself. It was one of the most difficult times of my life but I'm proud to say that I made it through as a happy, bright, and positive person. I still struggle with anxiety at times, but not as badly, and I have learned healthy coping mechanisms to help me deal with it. As I am writing this book, we are amid the 2020 Coronavirus pandemic, which has created a lot of anxiety for me because I was not able to go back home to Norway when the pandemic first hit. I had to stay in the States. I followed the steps that I learned from my therapist back in college and luckily, I have been able to lower my anxiety in the last few months.

Do you ever look inwards, without judgment or prejudice? Try to evaluate yourself without comparison to others. Be critical, write down the things that can be improved, and work on making those changes every day. It may sound rigorous, but if you do it every day it will become a healthy habit and part of your routine. Keep in mind that it takes 21 days to create or break a habit.

When you have a lot on your plate, it can be hard to focus on one thing. Your mind may tell you something that your heart doesn't believe. At times you may struggle with sleeping due to anxiety, and you have millions of questions running through your mind. If you find yourself doubting and questioning everything you do: drink herbal tea before sleep, take deep breaths, take a break from what you're doing and regroup.

You might have doubts about the future, what you're going to do next if you'll succeed in it. Will you be great at your sport? You have to remember that some things are not in our control. You cannot make someone love you or care about you, you can't control a car accident -

focus on the things you can control. If you treat anxiety as a guest who will visit for some time and will leave eventually, you will be at peace. If you view anxiety as a big dark cloud that is constantly pouring rain, your life will start going in that direction as you make anxiety your permanent companion. Remind yourself of your true inner power. Your beliefs and hopes define your life. Your anxiety can not control your life because you are the only one with hands on the steering wheel.

Here are some ways to cope with the anxiety that will prove to be helpful:

1. Calm Training

Calm training is an activity in which a group of people is taught to follow routines that will help their mind, body, and soul relax. The purpose of calm training is to relax performers. If you feel relaxed as a performer, you will eventually have less struggle in any event and be able to perform more effectively. There are two methods of calm training when it comes to sports performance. In the first method, training and competition settings are not related and you can relax while listening to your favorite music or attend yoga classes. In the second, you change the environment of the room before any competition. You can do this by using positive statements and calming the mind and body with breathing exercises and meditation.

2. Breathing Exercises

We often underestimate the power of deep breathing. If you face anxiety and want to get rid of it, the strategy of deep breathing can help. You can practice it from time to time to maximize its benefits. By practicing deep breathing, you will also be able to address various parts of your body. One simple breathing exercise that I have for you is to sit down on a flat surface, such as a workout or a yoga mat. Relax your mind. Close your eyes, and take a deep breath through your nose. Hold it there for a few seconds and then release it slowly from your mouth. Repeat until you feel yourself calming down. This breathing exercise works like magic when it comes to fighting anxiety, so practice often to master it.

3. Set Goals

This is a simple yet very useful technique when it comes to coping with anxiety. Imagine two people, A and B. A has everything figured out. They know what their goals are and what strategies they should be using to get closer to their goals with each passing day. B, on the other hand, has no idea what's going on and this is giving him anxiety. He is clueless about his next step and hasn't thought about what his goals are for the next two or five years. I will let you be the judge here and decide - who is more likely to reach their goal more easily? Yes, you guessed right – person A. My point here is that goal setting will help you to maintain a purposeful direction and focus on the tasks you have at hand. Make sure that you have set small goals for yourself so that you have a roadmap to help you reach your main goal.

4. Positive Self-Talk

You should practice positive self-talk regularly. I encourage you to do so because once you start doing it daily, over time you will see that your mind starts accepting it without even realizing it. Positive self-talk supports your perception of yourself within your mind. If your mind is positive and you practice being kind to yourself, you are more likely to lead a more balanced and successful life with minimal traces of anxiety. When you talk to yourself positively and treat yourself nicely, you are directing your thinking in a direction that will support your performance and you will be able to ace any competition. When you feed your mind with positive thoughts and you become your own biggest supporter, there will be no room left for anxiety.

5. Emotional Control

One of the qualities of excellent student-athletes includes understanding their levels of performance. You need to learn to recognize the feelings you get when you give a good performance. Identify these feelings and compare them to the ones you get after giving a poor performance. Doing this exercise will enable you to understand how you should respond and the way you should feel during emotional states that are changing constantly.

6. Question the Pattern of Your Thoughts

A contributor of problems and anxiety is negativity. It can make any situation feel severe very quickly. The best way to cope with this is to challenge your fears. Have a conversation with them; ask yourself if those fears are true and worth your time and thoughts. You will gain back control of your mind when you have this internal discussion. We tend to see challenging situations as being out of our control. This is not true. You cannot decide to lose before trying. You have to give it a go, and soon you will see the confidence booming inside you.

7. Aromatherapy

Aromatherapy is a great way to cope with anxiety. It soothes your soul as you take in the calming scents and relax your mind. You can choose aromatherapy in any form including oil, incense, or candles. Scents like

lavender, chamomile, and sandalwood have proven to be very helpful

in calming down a person's mind during anxious moments.

8. Write Down Your Thoughts

Writing can be another form of relieving stress and anxiety. If

something is bothering you and making you anxious, try writing it

down. Get it out of your system as soon as possible. This can feel

refreshing, make the situation less daunting, and you will feel more in

control once you've got it down on paper.

9. Exercise

When it comes to managing anxiety, exercise should be your go-to

solution. Exercise releases chemicals in your brain that boost your

mood and lower anxiety. It will also give you a break from your

worries and will help you work off that nervous energy, leaving you

relaxed and stress-free. I recommend that you add cardio exercise for a

half-hour a day three times a week to help combat anxiety.

"What is bad luck? Opinion. What are conflict, dispute, blame,

accusation, irreverence, and frivolity? They are all opinions, and more

than that, they are opinions that lie outside of our own reasoned choice, presented as if they were good or evil. Let a person shift their opinions only to what belongs in the field of their own choice, and I guarantee that person will have peace of mind, whatever is happening around them." —EPICTETUS, DISCOURSES, 3.3.18b–19

Don't put yourself under too much pressure. If you feel like a situation or a person is draining you, walk away. You don't have to respond to everything that is said to you. Similarly, you don't have to react to bad situations right away. Give yourself time to process and heal. If someone has hurt you or discouraged you, remind yourself of the victories you have won in the past, and that you've come out stronger. As soon as you notice symptoms of anxiety, which can include trembling, fast heartbeat, trouble sleeping or having an unsatisfied period of sleep, overthinking, over planning, and worrying too much about the future, you need to start addressing it. If you notice any of these symptoms, try using one or more of the tips listed above.

If you are not able to cope with your anxiety after trying everything mentioned above, I advise you to seek out a therapist, and there is nothing wrong with that. Attending therapy shows that you put yourself first and that you care to become the best version of yourself. Try to fight anxiety with the help of your inner self. If you succeed in following all of the above instructions carefully, then you will likely soon experience your last days with anxiety, so keep going and stay strong!

I have been through it myself, and using these methods will help you feel better. There will be numerous occasions when you may feel as though there is no way out, but trust me: there is always a way to reach hope and enlightenment. You have to believe in yourself, and tell yourself that you are stronger than your anxiety and that your anxiety cannot control you. I went through it with grace and dignity and I'm proud to say that thanks to my motivation, dedication, research, and support from my loved ones, I learned to cope with anxiety a lot sooner than expected.

"To live is not to breathe but to act. It is to make use of our organs, our senses, our faculties, of all the parts of ourselves which give us the sentiment of our existence. The man who has lived the most is not he who has counted the most years but he who has most felt life."
— **Jean-Jacques Rousseau**

Chapter 9

Organization/Efficiency

Have you heard of the "10,000-hour rule?" Malcolm Gladwell

conducted a study on the key to success, and the outcome showed the

average elite who mastered their skill spent around ten thousand hours

on their craft to become an expert. This amounts to working twenty

hours a week for ten years on your passion. To spend this much time on

a skill or to master anything, you need organization and efficiency.

Being organized plays a very important role in both academic and

athletic careers. Imagine walking into a messy room. You have no clue

where your books are and there are clothes everywhere. Without even

realizing it, your mind will begin to get frustrated and as a result, it will

reflect in your behavior. When you keep your room and workplace

clean and tidy, it will send a positive signal to your brain that

everything is placed perfectly and the tidiness will soothe you from

within. Cleanliness will make you feel relaxed and help you save time!

You don't want to lose or forget the things you need for practice,

competition, or tournaments when they're needed.

Do you know what experts say about motivation? They will tell you to make your bed first thing every morning. When you do this, you complete the first task of the day early on. It will give you confidence and motivation to do the next task and then the next. Making your bed is like placing a strong base for your day. I can confirm that this method works - it doesn't matter if I'm at a hotel or home but every morning when I wake up, I make my bed. I cannot leave unless all my pillows are perfectly set. It gives me a sense of organization in my life and it makes me feel like I can conquer anything that comes my way throughout the day. If you find that one thing in the morning that gives you a sense of clarity and organization, do it consistently and never let go. It will translate into the other areas of your life. Try practicing this every day and see the results for yourself. You cannot even imagine the kind of energy boost it will give you in the morning and the motivation you will feel.

Being an organized person is a blessing if you recognize it. Your life becomes much easier when you have organized a place and time for everything. Here are some habits you can work on to become more organized:

1. Stop Procrastinating

Procrastination can be our downfall. It is a fact that the longer we wait to get something done, the more difficult it will become later on. If you want to be an organized student-athlete and say goodbye to all the stress and demands, you have got to stop procrastinating. You must put effort toward your responsibilities as soon as possible and you will be released from the weight of doing it later on. This will open up time for rest, friends, and other extracurricular activities.

2. Write Things Down on a Paper

We are so lucky to live in a time where we have reminders that pop up to tell us it's someone's birthday. But back when cell phone reminders weren't around, people still remembered birthdays and sent cards for holidays? It wasn't magic - writing things down saves you a lot of time and regrets. There are two benefits of developing this habit – the first is you can see all the tasks of your day in one place and keep checking them off as you finish. This creates a sense of motivation as you complete one task after another. The second and most obvious benefit is that you never forget to get things done because there is no chance of forgetting!

3. Do Not Underestimate Making Deadlines and Schedules

Deadlines work like this: there's a sword hanging above your head, and you need to complete the task as soon as possible or you will have to face the consequences. Have you noticed how in workplaces, employees are under so much pressure to submit a report or attend a meeting by a certain time or date? This is because their bosses demand that they be on time and submit important reports by a given deadline. After all, timeliness is crucial to the overall performance of a business. College prepares you for that because your professors will demand that you meet all the deadlines for your assignments, and this can quickly become rigorous. While pursuing an athletic career, I highly recommend that you take your education seriously. I am a huge advocate for college because it provides an individual with critical thinking skills. You must remain productive and set personal deadlines and goals for the week. Most importantly, you must stick to these schedules and deadlines as they will work like magic to get your life organized and remove all the mess you don't need.

4. Give a Home to Everything

Another great way to become an organized person is to give a home to everything. If you want to keep your life organized, you must assign proper places to every item. You can do this by labeling your storage boxes (tip: never label anything as "miscellaneous!"). Try to get creative when it comes to organizing your home. Giving everything its proper place will make your home look neat and tidy. Furthermore, you will know where even the smallest things are located.

5. Keep What You Need and Discard the Rest

Have you heard of the minimalist lifestyle? It requires one to remove excess possessions; things that take space but have no value or purpose must be discarded. Embracing minimalism will allow you to enjoy your life more, and will declutter your home and your mind. What's the point of spending money on things you're never going to use? Instead, when you have fewer things you can enjoy them even more, rather than letting half of what you own be coated with dust. Be honest with yourself - what do you own that you really need or that truly means something to you? Keep those items, and get rid of the rest.

6. Declutter Regularly

Have you ever felt frustrated when you open your wardrobe and all the clothes fall on your feet? You curse those clothes for not being in place and tuck them in again. Instead of being frustrated with your clothes, try to change your habits and make it a habit to declutter regularly. Dedicate one or two days of the week to organizing your space. Your wardrobe, your kitchen cabinets – it can be anything. Your belongings won't organize themselves; you need to tend to them regularly and remain consistent to reduce clutter. Decluttering also makes you feel relaxed mentally. This doesn't just apply to physical things you can do this with the files on your computer, your phone gallery, and so on. So declutter, declutter and declutter!

7. Say No to Sale!

You have finally succeeded in decluttering and reorganizing your space but you open Instagram and there is a sale on Fashion Nova or Amazon. Are you going to replace the things you discarded with more clutter, or are you going to choose wisely? Instead of opting for an unplanned shopping spree, I recommend that you write down the things you truly need on paper and only buy those items - nothing else. Don't allow yourself to give in, and be as clever and patient as you can while shopping. This will save you a lot of money and clutter.

8. Be Aware of Where to Discard Items

Now that you have decluttered your space and made organized labeled boxes for everything, the question is where to discard everything you no longer want. Find charities and donate to a good cause. This way, your belongings will not go to waste and instead help someone in need.

The above-mentioned habits will help you get started organizing your life. If you stick to at least a few of these habits, you can live a life of freedom and intention. Organized people live more peacefully because they have rid themselves of the unnecessary. No delays, no procrastination, no clutter, and no mess. Their lives become easier as they remove mundane activities with the things they enjoy and love. You can do this, too, and you might just find that you get addicted to organizing.

Becoming efficient and organized is an investment in yourself. When you're organized at home, your mind will open up to new challenges and opportunities in sports. If you feel like going to Ikea and stocking up on storage boxes, then do it. Explore your creativity and always remember there is no pressure. Do it at your ease and comfort level. Best of luck!

What is your "why?" When you find it, it will lead you to your "how."

Chapter 10

Drive

What fuels your passion? What is the feeling that keeps you moving forward? Why would we invest in a sport knowing we could get injured, and possibly never reach our goal? Have you ever wondered how you became so capable of being consistent in your pursuit of success? The answer is drive.

Nothing in my life has happened based on luck. With a lot of grace, hard work, divine order, and blessings I was able to achieve my goals, though I'm still on my journey I recognize the order of my purpose. "Luck is preparation meeting the moment of opportunity." – Seneca.

At times, we may feel like procrastinating and delaying our daily tasks. These delays disrupt us from achieving targets that are supposed to take us closer to our goals. Everyone makes mistakes; no person before you has lived a life without mistakes. Drive works like a chain reaction. If you lack the willingness to do something, you will never be able to finish what you started. You have to learn how to use your drive, give everything you have, and believe in yourself so you can reach your truest potential. If you are serious about achieving your goals, you must focus on your drive. Remember that if you're procrastinating, it can only be for a short while – never make it a habit.

When you participate in a sport, you automatically become very driven and active. You seek opportunities to improve and start working as soon as you can. This is just what sports do to us. However, many situations can weaken our drive.

For example, you are practicing with your friend and she stops midway saying that she has had enough for the day. You remind her how important it is to keep going provided she has to play in a tournament soon. She shrugs it off and tells you she has more important things to do, and that she can practice later on. She goes home and you go home as well. But when you do, you keep thinking about what she said. You start thinking about how she's being easy on herself, and that maybe you could take it easy, too. Why are you taking the practice so seriously if she isn't? You will question yourself about taking breaks and eventually, you will soon start delaying practice or avoiding it. It starts to become a habit and without even realizing it, you have drifted far away from your goals.

Let me reframe the above situation and show you how it looks when your drive is strong. Your friend tells you that she can practice later, but instead of thinking about taking a break, you motivate yourself to work even harder and show her what she's missing. You take it as an opportunity to work harder to the extent that she starts feeling bad about it and joins you again! This is one of the ways to keep the drive alive in sports. If you want to become a successful student-athlete, you must keep in mind how important it is to be driven instead of taking it lightly.

"Those obsessed with glory attach their well-being to the regard of others, those who love pleasure tie it to feel, but the one with true understanding seeks it only in their actions...
. . Think on the character of the people one wishes to please, the possessions one means to gain, and the tactics one employs to such ends. How quickly time erases such things, and how many will yet be wiped away." —MARCUS AURELIUS, MEDITATIONS, 6:51, 59

Become excellent at your craft; it doesn't matter if you are a janitor, a cashier, an Uber driver, a doctor, a teacher, or a mailman. Your legacy lies in the impression you leave behind, so if you do an excellent job, people will remember your excellent work. It doesn't matter what your field of expertise is; what matters is your level of effort and the drive you possess.

It wasn't always easy for me as a black figure skater. I struggled with the most minor things, such as trying to find tights in my skin color. One year, I went to a dance store in my neighborhood to see if they had my skin color in figure skating tights, and they had one pair left. As a kid, I held onto those tights and prayed to God that they would not rip.

I had put in an order at the store and told them the exact color I needed for the tights. The lovely lady at the cash register seemed almost sad when she looked up at me and said, "Sorry, we don't have any more in stock and we don't know when we will have more in that exact color." In college, I used the dancewear brand Capezio, which was not even created for figure skating. I used to have to wear two tights to double them up; if I didn't, the tights were simply too thin, and at the rink which is kept below freezing at all times, using dance tights that are made for warm temperatures is not the best. I feel that figure skating brands specifically (tights manufacturers) often neglect that there are people of color who figure skate and I believe that we deserve to have tights available for purchase just like everyone else. It often made me feel excluded and sad. A couple of months after I had put in the order at the store for my specific tights, I got the call that they were back in stock.

I ran out of class and drove to Summerlin. I'm surprised I didn't get a speeding ticket, because between you and me I think I drove like a maniac that day just to get these tights before closing time. I felt that urgency because I had a competition that upcoming weekend and with all the schoolwork I had to do, this was my only opportunity to purchase the tights. When I got there I asked how many of the tights in my color she had, Carol said nine, and I bought seven of them. I wanted to buy them all, but a part of me thought maybe there is another black dancer that needs these tights in this color. The tights I bought that day lasted me almost two years, and I do compete a lot so that was a purchase I don't regret. If you are a black figure skater or dancer reading this, auroratights.com, discountdance.com, and Capezio.com have some great tights in all skin tones.

Thousands of people say they want to accomplish various goals every day, but why is there only one Elon Musk, Bill Gates, Mark Zuckerberg, Oprah Winfrey, Jeff Bezos? There are seven billion people on earth, but less than one percent will ever accomplish something so extraordinary. Why? Some may say lack of opportunity, dedication, vision, belief. Oprah was born in a small town near Nashville, was abused throughout her childhood, and still went on to become the greatest talk show host of all time and the first black female billionaire. How many people possess the drive to create something magical? Everything is possible if you have the drive and believe in yourself.

If you don't possess the drive to follow your passion, nobody and nothing can help you in achieving your goals. Signing yourself up for a tournament without giving one hundred percent of your effort will not only harm your reputation but also discourage your teammates who in one way or another, depend on you. If you want your team to be strong at the base, you need to make sure that your drive is alive in the sport you are playing. Be determined and focus on your prize, and you will find the motivation to keep giving it your all. Be a team player and motivate your teammates. Our energy is contagious, if you are slacking, or being lazy then you will receive that. The third law of physics states that as you work the energy you put out will return. It is already at work; recognize that you have a choice to do your best in every situation. This will encourage them and make your team stronger.

"Every habit and capability is confirmed and grows in its corresponding actions, walking by walking, and running by running . . .

therefore, if you want to do something make a habit of it, if you don't want to do that, don't, but make a habit of something else instead. The same principle is at work in our state of mind. When you get angry, you've not only experienced that evil, but you've also reinforced a bad habit, adding fuel to the fire." —EPICTETUS, DISCOURSES, 2.18.1–5

I admit that with all the chaos and responsibilities we have in our lives, it can be hard to focus on our goals. Sometimes anxiety and stress can take their toll and confuse you. You may feel like you can't manage everything on your plate all at once. This chaos can be very unhealthy for your athletic career. Here's a tip to set your head on straight and bring your drive back to life: write down where you started, what you're doing currently, and where you're supposed to be in the future. Note each step in your plan to reach your goal. You can add pictures and visuals for inspiration at each stage. This will help you see how far you've come already, and clarify and reinvigorate your future goals.

This activity is tried and tested. I did it first myself and after seeing the results I recommended it to my friends. They all did the same, and soon I could see a boost in the way they were training. The benefits of doing this activity include:

•Visualizing your final destination. This will create excitement in your heart and give you the motivation you need to reach your goal.

•Envisioning each step involved in your journey.

•Writing down the vision of your final destination and put the note away; do not open it again until you've accomplished your goal.

"Genius is one percent inspiration, ninety-nine percent perspiration." - Thomas Edison

Drive is one of the primary factors behind being successful. It signifies the strength of commitment a person feels toward achieving the objectives and goals they have set for themselves, thus you must devote yourself to keeping your drive high. You can ask any successful athlete the reason for their success and the first thing they will tell you is their drive and dedication. Drive is the ultimate key to becoming successful.

Drive consists of a mixture of hard work, dedication, and willingness to achieve your goals. *"Hard work is the key to success."* Yes, it requires physical practice but more than that it requires self-discipline, the right attitude, and the ability to remain focused on your target result. Things will get rough, and your body will become fatigued, but as a student-athlete, you must create a space in your mind where you can compartmentalize your sport and your schoolwork. To fully succeed, you can never let one or the other overwhelm you. The show must go on no matter how mentally or physically exhausted you get.

"You have to expect things of yourself before you can do them." -
Michael Jordan

Never be deterred by the failures you encounter. Instead, take them as opportunities to learn about your weaknesses and use them against your opponent in your next performance. During my freshman year, I used to imagine the day of my graduation, and how happy it would take me to complete my education with good grades while pursuing my passion of becoming the best figure skater I could be. I did it, and so can you. You have to make your mind and your choices a priority, be courageous and never look back, and immerse yourself in each moment.

To stay driven, you have to remain dedicated to your goal and work hard despite obstacles or failures. If you don't do well at a competition or lose at a tournament, the reality is that it's already in the past and you can start over and achieve better results next time. Look inward and reflect on how you can do better. Write your mistakes down in your phone or diary and ask yourself these questions: What did I mess up? Why did I pop that jump? Why did I miss that goal? Analyze your answers and then improve those mistakes next time. You have to eliminate the "what if I fail" question and just give one hundred percent of your efforts. Once you start thinking this way, your level of drive will increase and bring success your way.

Persistent effort and prioritizing what's most important will be your gateway to success. The more driven you are, the happier you will be. Many people in this world have dreams that require great exertion and strenuous hardships to be reached, and only a few of them will accomplish those dreams. That is why I challenge you to look deep within yourself and ask what you are willing to do to reach your goals. Never be afraid to try something, because it is okay to fail. Every day is a new opportunity for you to improve, you must approach everything with this mindset that today might be your last opportunity.

A skater once told me she likes trying to psyche out competitors by making noises while they're skating or making comments to them before they get on the ice, but that is weak behavior. I always wondered what satisfaction she felt from doing that deliberately to others. This issue isn't exclusive to figure skating; in other sports, players try to create a reaction in their opponent to try and throw them off their game, which ultimately is a mistake, because expending your energy like that will not help you perform. Focusing on the task at hand is what will put your emotions in the right place. I challenge you to be greater than your fear, and if you fail you can live the rest of your life knowing that you tried your best, rather than forever wondering if you could have achieved your goal. In hindsight, you can learn from your mistakes and your defeats, and apply the lessons you learned in other aspects of your life. As long as you try to accomplish your goals you can't lose because there is always something to gain from a loss.

There is no formula that you can follow to create drive. You have to identify your targets, identify challenges and obstacles, and adjust your goals. Once you have succeeded in identifying the challenges in your life, think about ways you can fight and overcome them. Do you want to know which qualities you need to have to overcome the difficulties in your life? Infinite fortitude, stoic resistance, and perseverance. These will strengthen your mind until it becomes capable of fighting anything that threatens your success. Once you have developed these strengths, your drive will reach new heights and you will be ready to take on even the biggest challenges.

Each day we are dying. I know it sounds harsh, but I hope that it encourages you to spend your time wisely. Find yourself, believe in yourself, and don't worry about others' opinions; all you need is to understand why you are driven to do the things you do. Lucius Annaeus Seneca was a philosopher who lived in the most exciting time of Roman history. In one of his letters he wrote: *"Tranquility can't be grasped except by those who have reached an unwavering and firm power of judgment--- the rest constantly fall and rise in their decisions, wavering in a state of alternately rejecting and accepting things. What is the cause of this back and forth? It's because nothing is clear and they rely on the most uncertain guide--- common opinion."* - Seneca, Moral Letters 95.57b-58a.

The drive I had in college helped me persevere through every challenge. If it wasn't for my realization that drive is equally as important as hard work in order to become successful, I can't imagine where I would be standing today. I learned this the hard way, so my goal here is to save you from struggling in high school or college while being a student-athlete. Drive is not an overly complicated concept. It comes from within you. Recognize it and take care of it. Keep it alive

for as long as possible during your education and sports career and you

will have a fulfilling experience.

The purpose of life is to love yourself, trust yourself, believe in yourself and be yourself.

-LOUISA WARWIN

Chapter 11

Confidence

Being confident is often underestimated. Sometimes we end up falling into the same pattern as everyone else without ever realizing that we are unique. Confidence is a sense of self-assuredness that comes from recognizing what makes you special. Your confidence has to radiate from within. It can't be dependent on your accomplishments, weight, money, or looks - all of that can be taken away in an instant - but your mind and confidence lay within yourself.

"Above all, it is necessary for a person to have a true self-estimate, for we commonly think we can do more than we really can."-- Seneca, *On TRANQUILITY OF MIND, 5.2*

Don't underestimate or overestimate yourself, but believe that you are capable of reaching new levels. Look within yourself to understand your true potential. Identify your power and your weaknesses. Once you understand who you are, you move quietly and with resilience. Allow yourself to grow in your own opinions and make your path, make a new wave, break barriers - the only opinion that matters is yours.

You will meet people who will try to bring you down and shatter your confidence. They do so because they want to feel powerful. Never let people have emotional control over you; it will cause more harm than good. The sad thing is that some toxic people are within our closest circles such as family members and friends. External influences such as social media can cause even more confusion and toxicity. A combination of toxic sources can cause you real damage. The good news is that your mind can protect you from everything once you learn how to control it, even if you end up on a stranded island or in jail (which I hope you never will!).

Many young children possess unique and beautiful qualities, but as they grow up their personality just doesn't live up to those qualities and they fade away in the crowd because it was never nurtured and valued. If you have a family that makes you stressed or makes your self-confidence low, take a stand for yourself every once in a while. You are not a punching bag; you have a personality of your own – your special purpose in this world. And that is enough validation.

"Holding onto anger is like drinking poison and expecting the other person to die" – Buddha.

Think wisely about who you allow into your life. You will eventually have to remove toxicity, so try to do so before it extracts too much energy from you. Listen to your gut feeling - it will be clear about who you should remove from your circle. Once you are in a clear headspace, you must let go of the bad feelings and the hurt they caused you. Don't internalize any negative things they may have said about or to you - holding onto those feelings will damage your confidence.

Sometimes when your confidence is low, you might feel like nobody is supporting you so you might as well just give up. Never listen to that voice. Your gifts are unique and nobody can fulfill your purpose in this world except you. How can you fulfill your purpose and contribute to the growth of this world if you listen to every negative comment or criticism thrown your way? Protect your energy at all costs.

If you do start feeling low and down on yourself, here are some ideas you can try to boost your self-esteem back up:

1# Create boundaries

#2 Go for walks in nature

#3 Journal your thoughts

#4 Avoid comparing yourself to others

"The unrestricted person, who has in hand what they will in all events, is free But anyone who can be restricted, coerced, or pushed into something against what they will is a slave." -- Epictetus, DISCOURSES, 4.1.128b-129a

At times we feel so low in confidence that we start seeking validation in others. You don't have to do that. Do what makes *you* happy. Your major in school should make you happy. School can be difficult and stressful, but if you don't smile when you think about the future you are creating for yourself, you are in the wrong field. If you don't feel passion or if you feel dissatisfied and sad, you're doing the everyday routine but you might as well be in jail because you are not in control of your freedom. You have become a slave to your field of work or sport.

You need to have confidence that comes from your own belief in yourself. Never make the mistake of comparing yourself to others. They are blessed in their ways, but you never know what they go through in their hearts! You have your purpose in this world. You can never be replaced and that's what makes you special. In my life, I've met many people who told me that I would never be able to achieve the things I dreamed of. I looked within myself and found the confidence and drive to prove them wrong by accomplishing my goals.

People can hurt you, but remember that you never have to react to them, let alone let them bring down your confidence. The problem I observed throughout my teenage and college life and the lives of others is that we don't set boundaries. Our culture and society make us believe that we do not have the authority to set boundaries for ourselves. It is considered rude, and some people may even portray it as a lack of manners. This is all wrong - setting boundaries for yourself is healthy. If someone is disturbing your peace, discouraging you, or criticizing you, the best thing you can do for yourself is set boundaries with them.

This way, even if people say hundreds of bad things to you, you will have higher ground and your confidence will remain intact. People will soon learn to respect your boundaries and instead of taking it as rudeness, they will feel embarrassed to bother you. Your personality will become strong, you will feel more confident and stay at peace.

Chapter 12

Conclusion

"Joy for human beings lies in proper human work. And proper human work consists in: acts of kindness to other human beings, disdain for the stirrings of the senses, identifying trustworthy impressions, and contemplating the natural order and all that happens in keeping with it." —MARCUS AURELIUS, MEDITATIONS, 8.26

If you asked me what I want you to take away from this book, there are three main teachings:

•Believe in yourself

•Follow your heart

•Be kind to yourself

I know that being a student-athlete in college is not a piece of cake. I encourage you to remember these key lessons and never let them go. Write them down in pretty fonts, print them out, and stick them on your vision board.

"You say, good fortune used to meet you at every corner. But the fortunate person is the one who gives themselves good fortune. And good fortunes are a well-tuned soul, good impulses and good actions."
—MARCUS AURELIUS, MEDITATIONS, 5.36

Believe in your vision, not other people's perceptions of your vision. They might not understand your vision in the first place. I strongly encourage you to hold onto your vision, whether or not you have external support. Do it for you. Muhammed Ali became the greatest boxer of all time solely because he followed his vision for his career. Michelle Kwan became a five-time world champion, a nine-time U.S nationalist, and a two-time Olympian. This type of courage and dedication is unmatched, but she followed her dreams and most of all, her heart. Surya Bonaly was the first woman to ever land a backflip on the ice in history; the number of people that told her not to do it was immeasurable, but had she listened to them she would not have made history.

Nothing feels better than doing what you love and following your heart. Trust yourself, because you will never fail if you follow your heart's desire with dedication and a positive mindset. If you love something and want to do it even if the whole world is against it, do it. If it doesn't work out, you will have no regrets and will learn valuable lessons in the process. But if it does, the rest of the world will look in silence and admire your dedication towards your accomplishment. There are so many business icons, celebrities, and scientists in this world who listened to their hearts and followed their dreams.

Today, they have taken over the world with amazing technology, businesses, contributions to the arts, and development. These personalities include Steve Jobs, Albert Einstein, Thomas Edison, Shakespeare, and so many more. Never give in to others' opinions of your talents and capabilities, and never let them affect your confidence in a negative way.

Please, remember to be kind to yourself. I learned this the hard way - that's why I want you to remember this no matter what happens. Always put your physical and mental health first, and the rest comes later.

In the end, health is wealth. If you are not kind to yourself, not taking care of your health, and always thinking bad thoughts about yourself, how will you gain the confidence to stand with the rest of the world? You need to feed your mind and body with positivity so that you are healthy at heart and physically fit. Do not be afraid to ask for resources at your university, because it is their job to guide you when you feel that you are lost.

There is no shame in seeking help. Student counseling can be very helpful to deal with stress and anxiety. Think of it as an escape from all the negativity, as you pour it all out and reduce the weight that is on your heart.

I have considered a lot while writing this book, so it speaks nothing but my truth. I aim to help student-athletes like you as much as I can and make their lives easier. The tips and methods I have written about will help you get through your most difficult times. Being a student-athlete is an experience you will cherish for the rest of your life.

This book is a guide for you to become the best student-athlete you can while grappling with the tough scenarios you may face along the journey. Hopefully, you can look to this book as a guiding light in your academic and athletic career and encourage you to be your truest self. You have all my support and best wishes as you work to become a successful student-athlete of the future!

Good Luck,

Louisa Warwin

I would like to say a big thank you to family, coaches, friends, and all the faculty at Vanguard University who have supported me throughout my journey.

Cited

Aristotle, and W. D. Ross. Nicomachean Ethics. Book I.

Generic NL Freebook Publisher, 2000. EBSCOhost,

search.ebscohost.com/login.aspx?direct=true&db=n

lebk&AN=1085829&site=ehost-live&scope=site.

Epictetus, , George Long, and Epictetus. The Discourses of

Epictetus: With the Encheiridion and Fragments.

London: G. Bell and Sons, 1916.

Marcus Aurelius, Emperor of Rome, 121-180. The

Meditations of Marcus Aurelius. Mount Vernon

[N.Y.] :Peter Pauper Press, 194